ASSESSING AND RECORDING ACHIEVEMENT

ASSESSING ASSESSMENT

Series Editor:
Harry Torrance, University of Sussex

The aim of this series is to take a longer term view of current developments in assessment and to interrogate them in terms of research evidence deriving from both theoretical and empirical work. The intention is to provide a basis for testing the rhetoric of current policy and for the development of well-founded practice.

Current titles

Christopher Pole: *Assessing and Recording Achievement*
Malcolm Ross *et al.*: *Assessing Achievement in the Arts*

ASSESSING
ASSESSMENT

ASSESSING AND RECORDING ACHIEVEMENT

IMPLEMENTING A NEW APPROACH IN SCHOOL

Christopher J. Pole

Open University Press
Buckingham · Philadelphia

Open University Press
Celtic Court
22 Ballmoor
Buckingham
MK18 1XW

and
1900 Frost Road, Suite 101
Bristol, PA 19007, USA

First Published 1993

A catalogue record of this book is available from the British Library

Library of Congress Cataloging-in-Publication Data

Pole, Christopher J. (Christopher John), 1959–
    Implementing records of achievement/Christopher J. Pole.
        p.   cm.
    Includes bibliographical references and index.
    ISBN 0–335–09961–0 (hb.) ISBN 0–335–09960–2 (pb.)
    1. Student records — Great Britain — Case studies.   I. Title.
LB2845.7.P65   1993
371.2′7′0941 — dc20
                                                        92–18995
                                                            CIP

Typeset by Colset Pte Ltd, Singapore
Printed in Great Britain by Biddles Ltd, Guildford and Kings Lynn

For Jacqueline and Charlotte

CONTENTS

SERIES EDITOR'S INTRODUCTION

Changing theories and methods of assessment have been the focus of significant attention for some years now, not only in the United Kingdom, but also in many other western industrial countries and many developing countries. Curriculum developers have realized that real change will not take place in schools if traditional paper-and-pencil tests, be they essay or multiple choice, remain unchanged to exert a constraining influence on how teachers and pupils approach new curricula. Similarly, examiners have been concerned to develop more valid and 'authentic' (to use the American parlance) ways of assessing the changes which have been introduced into school syllabuses over recent years – more practical work, oral work, problem solving and so forth. In turn psychologists and sociologists have become less concerned with the practice and consequences of selection and more concerned with the impact of assessment on learning and motivation, and how that impact can be developed more positively. This has led to a myriad of developments in the field of assessment, usually involving an increasing role for the teacher in school-based assessment, as more relevant and challenging tasks are devised by examination agencies for administration by teachers in schools, and as the role and status of more routine teacher assessment of coursework, practical work, groupwork and so forth has become enhanced.

However, educationists have not been the only ones to focus much more closely on the interrelation of curriculum, pedagogy and assessment. Governments around the world, but particularly in the UK, have also begun to take a close interest in the ways in which assessment can influence and even control teaching, and in the changes in curriculum and teaching which could be brought about by changes in assessment. This interest has not been wholly coherent. Government intervention in the UK has sometimes initiated, sometimes reinforced the move towards a more practical and vocationally oriented curriculum and thus the move towards more practical, school-based assessment. But government has also been concerned with issues of accountability and with what it sees as the maintenance of traditional academic standards through the use of externally set tests.

It is precisely because of this complexity and confusion that the present series of books on assessment has been developed. Many claims are being made with respect to the efficacy of new approaches to assessment which require careful review and investigation. Likewise many changes are being required by government intervention which may lead to hurried and poorly understood developments being implemented in schools. The aim of this series is to take a longer term view of the changes which are occurring, to move beyond the immediate problems of implementation and to interrogate the claims and the changes in terms of broader research evidence which derives from both theoretical and empirical work. In reviewing the field in this way the intention of the series is thus to identify key factors and principles which should underpin the developments taking place, and provide teachers and administrators with a basis for informed decision-making which takes the educational issues seriously and goes beyond simply accommodating the latest policy imperative – difficult as even that has been in recent years!

With these intentions in mind, Christopher Pole's book is a particularly timely one. Although Records of Achievement, at least in the way they were conceived by UK government in the 1980s, have been demoted on the policy agenda, they remain a significant development with much potential still to be explored. And despite much debate and extensive evolution most of what is in print concerning Records of Achievement remains exhortatory and advocatory. The British government's own evaluation of its funded developments (the

PRAISE Report) provides important evidence of problems and benefits, but because it was focused on DES-funded schemes, questions
remain about more routine developments in 'ordinary' schools.
Christopher Pole offers us an account of Records of Achievement in
one such school and an account which provides evidence of the practice and effects of a Record of Achievement scheme which had
developed over some years and was operating throughout the school.
Of course no single study can serve for all Record of Achievement
experience, and Pole recognizes the importance of contextualizing
his data so that readers can make judgements about how similar or
different are their own situations, but 'Benton School' does provide
an interesting test case of the claims of the Record of Achievement
movement, particularly with respect to the whole-school nature of
the endeavour, and especially in the close attention which Pole pays
to the responses of pupils.

Much of the rhetoric of Records of Achievement revolved around
debates about target setting, dialogue and the promotion of learning. Much of the critique revolved around the possibilities for the
surveillance of pupils. Pole demonstrates that the reality is more
mundane but also more challenging in that there seems to be an
almost irresistible pressure to bureaucratize the process of recording
achievement in order for it to become integrated into the routines of
schooling. This bureaucratization blunts the worst threats of surveillance but also undermines much of the educational promise. Such
findings also beg questions about how we might institutionalize other
developments in assessment in schools – properly integrating assessment with teaching, for example, in the context of teacher assessment – without similarly over-bureaucratizing the whole process.

Pole's study raises important questions about the various purposes
of assessment; the point at which aspirations towards more holistic
assessment become over-complex and intrusive; the different
audiences which reports have to serve; and, perhaps most important
of all, the limits to pupil responsibility which are embedded not only
in the practices of schooling but also in the concepts and definitions
of teaching which underpin these practices. What emerges is a cau-
tionary tale for those who might believe that schools are easily
changed or easily controlled by changes in assessment. What also
emerges however is a range of interesting evidence and a number of
key factors which those school personnel who may be responsible for
developing a school's policy on assessment ought to find of value.

Harry Torrance

PREFACE AND ACKNOWLEDGEMENTS

This book grew out of a research and evaluation project in Records of Achievement conducted for Warwickshire Local Education Authority (LEA) by The Centre for Educational Development, Appraisal and Research (CEDAR) at the University of Warwick. The fieldwork upon which the book is based was made possible by a grant from Warwickshire LEA who also seconded two teachers to the project during the research period. The project has, therefore, been a collaborative venture between the LEA and CEDAR.

The book takes a case study approach and documents the Record of Achievement process in one school. It portrays the issues and concerns of those involved in the process, namely the teachers and the pupils. Throughout the case study the words of the teachers and pupils have been used to convey these concerns and issues and in doing this a context has been provided within which the Record of Achievement process may be viewed. The context is that of the school and the actors therein.

Data for the study were collected principally by means of tape-recorded interviews and discussions and also by observations conducted throughout Benton School. Seventeen members of staff were interviewed individually and 47 pupils took part in tape-recorded discussions, usually in pairs.

Throughout the study pseudonyms are used for all staff and pupils. The name of the school, Benton, is also a pseudonym. The conduct of this kind of detailed work requires assistance and co-operation from many people. I am particularly indebted, therefore, to the Head, the staff and pupils of Benton School, for their co-operation with my work and for allowing me to place yet another call on their time.

The support of Professor Robert Burgess and of the two seconded teachers, Keith Evans and Christine Priestley in discussing and drafting this volume has been invaluable. Thanks are also due to Harry Torrance for his helpful editorial comments.

The whole project was fortunate to have the secretarial support of Barbara Muldowney who also typed this manuscript. Any errors or omissions, however, remain my own.

INTRODUCTION

In January 1984 The Department of Education and Science (DES) issued a statement of policy on Records of Achievement. The statement outlined four key areas where the DES expected Records of Achievement to make a positive contribution towards the experience of schooling and represented the first official backing for such a reporting and recording process from a government department. Although various committees and reports (e.g. Norwood 1941; Newsom 1963) had called for a means of recording pupil progress, which went beyond the merely summative, it was not until 1984 that the DES gave official support to the development of Records of Achievement in England and Wales. The four key areas where they believed Records of Achievement would make a positive contribution to schooling were as follows:

1 *Recognition of achievement* – Records and recording systems should recognize, acknowledge and give credit for what pupils have achieved and experienced, not just in terms of public examinations but in other ways as well.
2 *Motivation and personal development* – They should contribute to pupils' personal development and progress by

improving their motivation, providing encouragement and increasing their awareness of strengths, weaknesses and opportunities.

3 *Curriculum and organization* – The recording process should help schools to identify the all-round potential of their pupils and to consider how well their curriculum, teaching and organization enable pupils to develop the general, practical and social skills which are to be recorded.

4 *A document of record* – Young people leaving school or college should take with them a short, summary document of record which is recognized and valued by employers and institutions of further and higher education. This should provide a more rounded picture of candidates for jobs or courses than can be provided by a list of examination results, thus helping potential users to decide how candidates could best be employed, or for which jobs, training schemes or courses they are likely to be suitable.

(DES 1984: 3)

The expectations which the DES had of Records of Achievement in terms not only of the reporting and recording process within schools, but also of their impact upon teaching and learning styles suggests that they were clearly more than just a new style of school report. Furthermore, numerous writers and researchers working in the field of Records of Achievement (e.g. Broadfoot 1982, 1986; Burgess and Adams 1985; Hitchcock 1986a,b) have drawn attention to what they see as the great potential for Records of Achievement to bring about change in schools. Burgess and Adams (1985: 76) offer the following exhortation:

It is potentially the most important national initiative in education since the establishment of a national system of public examination and it offers more hope than the latter for the enhancing of educational experience and standards.

A view of Records of Achievement which sees them as the most important education initiative since public examinations, attributes a great deal to a reporting document originally conceived by Sir Keith Joseph as a means of providing some kind of certification for the less able (James 1989a). Furthermore, reports from the Pilot Records of Achievement in Schools Evaluation (PRAISE 1987,

1988), established after the 1984 DES statement of policy, saw Records of Achievement providing a challenge to schools and to teachers. The reports based on a comprehensive data collection saw Records of Achievement in terms of instruments or catalysts for change in schools across a wide range of issues. The final report (PRAISE 1988: 178) made the following statement:

> Records of Achievement pose a challenge to schools and teachers that is perhaps unprecedented in formal education. They make novel and substantial demands on time, energy, resources and skill across a wide range of fronts – demands that schools and LEA have been able to meet to varying degrees.

By the end of the 1980s the rhetoric of Records of Achievement as the bringers of change in schools was well established. Much of the literature in the area was concerned with how to implement and develop the Record of Achievement within and throughout a school (e.g. Garforth and Macintosh 1986; Hitchcock 1986a; Broadfoot 1987; Evans 1988; Law 1988). However, apart from the official reports of PRAISE and associated local evaluation reports which were funded either directly or indirectly by the DES (e.g. ILEA 1988) there existed little in terms of objective, independent detailed accounts of user perspectives on Records of Achievements. Extravagant predictions about the likely impact of Records of Achievement on schools, teachers, pupils, parents and employers had been repeatedly made, yet the literature was devoid of any systematic school based study of Records of Achievement which could document their effect on any of these, or on classroom practices, teacher–pupil relations and definitions of achievement. In this sense, the study reported in this volume is intended to fill that gap.

In 1988, CEDAR at the University of Warwick was invited to conduct a study of the introduction and development of Records of Achievement within one LEA. The study was based on four case studies of different kinds of schools (Evans 1989; Pole 1989, 1991; Priestley 1990) each with different experiences of the Record of Achievement process, different kinds of expectations of it and different kinds of commitment to it.

This volume is based on one of those four case studies (Pole 1989) and provides insight into the experiences of teachers and pupils as they worked with Records of Achievement in the context of a small secondary High School. Data for the study were gathered by means of observations within the school and by tape-recorded interviews with pupils and teachers. The actual words of the pupils and teachers are used extensively throughout this volume and in effect it is an attempt to tell their story, to relate the actual user perspective in relation to the Records of Achievement experience. In this sense it is a subjective account. Fieldwork for the study was conducted over a period of four months (one school term) during which I spent a great deal of time in the school talking, observing, listening and learning about Records of Achievement policies and practices.

An opportunity to relate these experiences does indeed appear timely. In February 1991 the then Education Secretary, Kenneth Clarke, together with former Employment Secretary, Michael Howard, launched a National Record of Achievement (DES 1991). The secretaries of state in launching a National Pilot Record of Achievement, tied together the outcomes of the emerging National Curriculum and the needs of industry. They stated:

> The National Record of Achievement will become the vehicle for telling employers and others exactly what the school leaver's National Curriculum achievements have been.

Whilst use of the National Record of Achievement is to remain, for the time being optional, the government clearly intend to encourage schools and colleges to use the document.

> We want everyone to have a go at using it. We are going to make a point of following up reactions to it over the coming months.

Anticipating their follow-up of reactions the secretaries of state believe that the National Record of Achievement

> . . . will evolve and develop over time in the light of users' own practical experience of it.

Within a context of educational change which identifies a Record of Achievement as an important means of linking National Curriculum to the needs of industry, the study recounted in this volume offers an opportunity to do precisely what the government intends to do. That is, to examine teachers' and pupils' own practical experiences of constructing and using a Record of Achievement, to 'follow it up'.

1

SETTING THE SCENE

Although many claims have been made by the DES and others about the potential for Records of Achievement to bring about change in schools (e.g. DES 1984; Burgess and Adams 1985; RANSC 1989) little attention has been paid to the different kinds of schools within which Records of Achievement have been developed. The kinds of changes anticipated by the DES and others go beyond the reporting and recording mechanisms which schools might employ, to make challenges to the very nature of schooling, to school organization, to teacher–pupil relations and the very definition of achievement. Given such claims it seems likely that the impact of Records of Achievement will not be uniform across all schools but will vary in accordance with the type of school into which they are introduced.

In this respect the effects which Records of Achievement bring to bear on a school will be tempered by the range of social factors, educational and organizational criteria which the school possesses. For example, the size of the school, its location and the nature of its catchment area, together with its policies, should they exist, on reporting and recording, its structure and organization may all influence the extent to which Records of Achievement may become integrated with its activities and accordingly, the changes which they may bring. It is important in this first chapter, therefore, to set the scene for this case study of one school's experience of Records of Achievement, to provide the context and to convey something of the nature and flavour of the school. Against this, the impact of the Record of Achievement may more usefully be viewed.

Benton School

Benton School is a three-form entry 12–16 High School. Under the selective procedures operated in the Eastern district of its LEA, the school's intake consists of those pupils who have failed to qualify for a place in one of the local grammar schools. Consequently, the school does not cater for the top 20 per cent of pupils in the area, and although described as a High School its status is the same as that of the traditional Secondary Modern School established after the 1944 Education Act.

The school was small with 288 pupils on roll in the Spring term 1988–89. However, falling rolls were not a major issue as numbers had remained more or less constant in the past five years (Table 1). The pupil population was split more or less evenly between male and female in each of the four years. Pupils transferred to the school at the age of 12 from a large number of middle schools located in surrounding villages. Although they formed the youngest age group in the school they were referred to as second years. They remained at the school for a period of four years before leaving for further education at an LEA sixth form, Further Education (FE) College or the labour market.

Table 1   Benton School pupil numbers, Summer term 1989

	Boys	*Girls*	*Total*
2nd year	39	35	74
3rd year	38	36	74
4th year	40	37	77
5th year	34	29	63
Total	151	137	288

(Data provided by school office)

The physical structure of the school was small comprising of one main block, built in 1956 which housed most of the teaching rooms, staffroom and offices. The main block which had three floors had received various additions over time. In particular, new areas had been added during the 1970s for Craft, Design and Technology (CDT) and for Home Economics.

There were extensive playing fields, sufficient to house several football, rugby and hockey pitches, and during the summer a cricket square and athletics track. There was also a hard surface for netball and other sports. The staff car park was small and parking on the grassed areas which surrounded the car park was common. Pupils could bring bicycles to school and some cycle sheds were provided. Although there were sufficient sheds for all cyclists, many bicycles could be seen against the school railings or laid down on the grassed areas. In many cases the bicycles were left without a padlock.

Internally the school was in reasonable repair. Graffiti was not common and notice-boards and displays of pupils' work gave the main corridor some interest and an idea of the kinds of activities in which the school encouraged its pupils to take part. In particular, information about extra-curricular activities could be found on the notice-boards, for example fund raising and charity events, schools trips, sports teams, careers and work experience information. Generally, the school appeared bright and welcoming to the visitor and presumably to staff and pupils.

The catchment area

The semi-rural location of the school meant that its pupils were drawn not only from the village of Benton itself but also from the middle schools in many of the surrounding villages. The catchment area was, therefore, spread over a wide geographical area and as a result, approximately 170 pupils were bussed to and from the school each day.

As a consequence of the bussing and the location of the school, its social class composition was fairly heterogeneous. For example, pupils were drawn from a variety of areas which incorporated a range of different kinds of housing stock, including local authority, private modern estates and older more established developments. Pupils from traditional working-class families and more affluent middle-class backgrounds were, therefore, represented in the school. However, despite the mixed housing patterns in the school's catchment area, the organization of secondary schooling on the basis of selection in the LEA meant that those pupils from the most middle-class homes attend the grammar schools in the area. Nevertheless, the location of the school did provide greater heterogeneity than a traditional neighbourhood secondary modern or even a neighbourhood comprehensive. The school had only one immediate competitor for many of its pupils, and the scarcity of effective public transport in the area made travel to other schools difficult.

Benton School also drew pupils from rural and urban areas. Pupils travelled from the outskirts of a medium-sized town in addition to areas which were comparatively isolated and founded predominantly on their relationship with local agriculture.

The staff

The school had a total of 29 members of staff which included one headteacher, one deputy headteacher, 15 full-time teachers and four part-time teachers. The remainder of the staff were part-time clerical and technical assistants.

The small number of staff had implications for many different aspects of the school's organization, management, curriculum and timetable. In effect, the whole ambiance of the school and its approach to education was to a large extent determined by its size.

For example, the number of staff affected the size of teaching groups and the variety of different subjects available to pupils (cf. DES 1985). The number of pupils and staff was also seen to affect the range of extra-curricular activities offered by the school, for example Nick Reilley, a PE teacher at Benton, expressed concern over the difficulty in getting sufficient pupils and staff to run school sports teams. Responsibility for organizing the teams tended to fall to the same few staff every year and at the same time the school did not have large numbers of pupils with ability in football, rugby, hockey or netball.

A more positive aspect of this small school, however, was found in the fact that pupils and teachers had more opportunity to get to know each other. For example, most teachers taught most of the pupils in the school over the course of a week, in some cases for several periods. When staff had been at the school for several years they were able to develop a relationship with pupils over their entire time in the school.

Furthermore, virtually every member of staff taught more than one subject and usually taught across the entire age range. In some cases staff taught more than two subjects. Some felt this placed unrealistic demands on them and feared that they lacked sufficient depth of knowledge in some subject areas. The following extract from an interview with Susan Watts, a part-time teacher, demonstrated the versatility required of most Benton staff.

> SW: I teach .9 of the timetable which includes being in charge of the History department, teaching fifth-year GCSE Social Science groups, a fifth-year GCSE English group and co-ordinating and working with special needs as well.
>
> CP: That's a lot isn't it?
>
> SW: Yes an awful lot of responsibility. Yes, because I have three different exam groups with three different sets of course work and two of those areas are my responsibility.

Although the example of Susan Watts is probably the most extreme amongst the Benton staff, it serves to illustrate that a small school demands versatile staff who are able to offer a wide range of subjects. Furthermore, the size of the school had an obvious effect on department structure and size. One or two person departments were not uncommon in the school. At the same time, a head of department may also function as a head of year. Shirley Price, for example, in addition to her role as head of both second year and fifth year was also responsible for organization of Geography throughout the school and shared responsibility for organizing and teaching girls PE and games. She also taught boys PE and games, and English. All of these different roles brought their pressures and demands. She described her job in the following terms:

> It's like being in air-traffic control here. There are so many things buzzing around, and every now and then you pluck something down and do something with it.

Shirley Price was, therefore, head of one department, Geography, and a member of two others, PE and English. It may not be unconnected that my first contact with Shirley was a conversation held in the staffroom when she was searching for an aspirin for a headache!

It was in this context of a small rural school that this research into the development of Records of Achievement was carried out. Benton provided an excellent opportunity to examine the impact of the Record of Achievement, its development and the experiences of staff and pupils. The fact that the school was small was important as this meant that teachers and pupils had the potential to get to know each other better than in larger schools. For example, the fact that all Benton teachers taught in more than one subject area, most were form tutors and also engaged in some kind of extra-curricular and out-of-school activities meant there were many occasions when pupils would come into contact with the same teachers. In the context of Records of Achievement, such regularity of pupil–teacher contact could be seen as an aid to meaningful dialogue between the two parties. With teachers and pupils having the opportunity to get to know each other in a variety of situations the size of the school was conducive to the closer and more open teacher–pupil relations which the Record of Achievement process both necessitated and sought to foster. If this was the case, then Records of Achievement could be said to have something of a 'head start' in Benton School.

The fact that Records of Achievement had been in operation in Benton School for approximately five years by the time the research commenced is also important in the context of this case study. Benton was one of the few schools with a history of Records of Achievement. It had encountered many of the difficulties and problems which schools face when seeking to introduce Records of Achievement, the procedures had evolved over a period of five years and in many respects were a reflection of the problems that had been encountered. Clearly, Records of Achievement were of central importance to many of the staff and they seemed to underpin the head's philosophies of holistic education and formative assessment. At the same time, they had become the expected means of recording and reporting for many parents. To arrive at this position, the Benton Record of Achievement had been reviewed, modified and developed. It was by no means a static set of procedures or documents. It was, however, an established process.

Owing to its five-year history, therefore, Benton School provided something of a test case, not in terms of comparing other schools and Records of Achievement with it, but in terms of its own achievements. Despite the difficulties and doubts Benton School had developed and operated a Record of Achievement over a period of five years. The problems which remained with it when this research was conducted were not, therefore, teething problems. It seemed more likely that they were problems of an enduring nature, probably inherent to the type of school and the very nature of Records of Achievement. It seemed unlikely that they were problems which further development would automatically overcome. In this sense, Benton School provided an excellent opportunity for an evaluative case study.

Having provided this general background information it will now be useful to consider the Record of Achievement process which was operated within this context and to give some account of its history within Benton School.

The Record of Achievement process

The Record of Achievement process in Benton School centred around planned one-to-one discussion sessions between pupils and form tutors. During the sessions the strengths and weaknesses of the pupils were discussed, their achievements recognized and areas for further development were identified. Discussions between tutors and pupils could often be of a very personal nature, relating to pupils' home and out-of-school activities in addition to their performance at school. Consequently an effective rapport between tutor and pupil was essential.

To facilitate discussion of school activities the pupil was required to complete a pro-forma (Appendix 1) which listed statements (descriptors) about school activities. For example, reading, number work and understanding. The statements related to levels of achievement in these activities. Members of staff with whom the pupil had contact, usually for specific lessons, completed the same proforma (descriptor sheet) prior to the one-to-one discussion between pupil and form tutor. The completed descriptor sheets were collected by the form tutor and then provided the basis for the discussion of the pupil's progress during the one-to-one session.

The introduction and continued development of Records of Achievement in Benton School could be attributed in many respects to the headteacher, David Fox. At the outset it was his interest in the philosophy of formative recording together with a dissatisfaction with the reporting system that existed in the school which spurred an initial attempt at a Record of Achievement in the school. In addition, support from two senior staff in the school provided a commitment to their further development (cf. Saunders 1986 and Technical and Vocational Education Initiative (TVEI) enclaves).

Initial attempts at the Record of Achievement were made on a very limited scale with one fifth-year group. The success of this 'pilot' created interest throughout the school and amongst officers of the LEA. Continued advances in school led to support from the LEA to further develop the Record and to funding from an FE college to develop a computer program for descriptors and comment banks.

Although not all teachers at Benton School were immediately convinced of the benefits of the Record of Achievement, the commitment of the head, the deputy and a third senior member of staff, together with the growing interest in the scheme from outside the school, created a momentum towards their development on a whole-school basis. Benton's experiences became well known throughout the LEA, the head and other staff contributed to the wider development of Records of Achievement in other schools, through provision of In-Service Education and Training (INSET) and by sharing their experiences. In this sense the head and several other Benton staff have been influential in shaping the Record of Achievement in several schools within the LEA. Notably, the original list of descriptors for use in the teacher–pupil discussion sessions were developed by Benton staff in conjunction with LEA officers with a view to their dissemination and use throughout the LEA.

Funding for this was provided through the LEA TVEI grant. The influence that the Benton experience had brought to other schools in the same LEA, again made Benton an interesting and important location for a case study.

One of the main objectives of the discussion sessions was to produce a set of statements (descriptors), which were agreed by the tutor and the pupil, which adequately and fairly described the progress and achievements of the pupil over the preceding school year. One-to-one discussion sessions in Benton School were scheduled to last for approximately 30 minutes and occurred at least once each year. The sessions were intended, therefore, to consider the progress of the pupil from one discussion session to the next and to identify points for development. To reach agreement over the selection of descriptors, pupils and tutors were frequently involved in what was described as negotiation. Consequently 'negotiation sessions' had evolved as the term most frequently used by staff and students to describe the one-to-one discussion.

Most groups of descriptors were arranged in hierarchies and levels of achievement were illustrated by the descriptor agreed upon by pupil and tutor. Negotiation occurred, therefore, when there were discrepancies between tutor and pupil over the choice of a descriptor. The result was often a compromise between the two, before an agreed set of descriptors could be reached.

During negotiation sessions pupils and teachers identified specific goals which pupils would seek to achieve during the course of the coming school year. Goals could relate to school work and activities; for example, to improve handwriting, to make a greater effort with homework. Equally they could relate to out-of-school activities; for example, to join a youth club, to give more assistance with household chores. The pupil made an undertaking to seek to achieve the goals and progress made was discussed during a review or updating session later in the same academic year.

Various reporting mechanisms were built into the Benton Record of Achievement programme which provided parents with information about the progress of their children. They also allowed parents to contribute to the Record of Achievement process by commenting on the behaviour of their children at home and on leisure activities. The intention was to make parents and out-of-school activities part of the totality of the reporting and recording process.

In short, the Record of Achievement process, although designed to encourage pupil–teacher interaction and to accommodate the needs of the individual pupil, followed a well-structured path. Thus:

- Subject teachers' complete descriptor sheets on each of their pupils.
- Descriptor sheets are collected from each subject teacher by the form tutor. The form tutor then completes a descriptor sheet based on the information provided by subject teachers.
- Each pupil completes a descriptor sheet giving his or her view of the same qualities commented on by the staff.
- Form tutor and pupil meet for a discussion session. The descriptor sheets completed by the form tutor and the pupil are

compared. Discussion and, where necessary, negotiation takes place between tutor and pupil in order to produce a joint statement of pupil Achievement and progress. Goals and targets are discussed and set. Teacher and pupil sign an agreed document which makes a statement of the pupil's progress and details the goals.

- An 'Up-date' meeting between tutor and pupil takes place to review progress made on goals and targets.
- Reports to parents are a summary produced from the process showing overall grades and achievements, but not teacher comments or information relating to individual subjects. Parents are asked to complete a pro-forma commenting on their child's progress and on the Record of Achievement itself. They may also provide information on home and out-of-school activities.

The process was essentially the same for all pupils in the school. Descriptor sheets (Appendix 1) were, however, changed between third and fourth years to take account of the development and greater maturity of pupils. Also information about pupils' activities in the home, for example, about their contribution to household chores such as washing up, making beds, etc. was requested only during the second and third years. The head and deputy argued that information of this nature aided the school in forming a more complete picture of the pupil which may be useful in goal-setting exercises, and could help teachers in their pastoral role. However, not all staff found this section of the record helpful, and some parents saw it as an invasion of privacy.

Both the head and most Benton staff identified the most important element of the process as the one-to-one discussion sessions between teacher and pupil. The completion of descriptor sheets by teachers and pupils was in many ways merely a means of facilitating the negotiation and discussion. The qualities, skills and abilities with which the descriptor sheets were concerned served to provide a basis for discussion, and an aid to the identification of strengths and weaknesses which were important for the development of the pupil. The descriptors could also be useful in the identification of goals and targets by teachers and pupils. During negotiation sessions teachers and pupils were concerned not merely with the qualities and abilities as they were specified by the descriptors but with the way in which collectively the descriptors produced a picture of 'the whole' pupil.

In this respect discussion during negotiation sessions frequently strayed from the descriptors to wider concerns of the pupil, including both in school and out of school activities.

In the fourth and fifth year agreed statements between tutor and pupil were entered into a computer data base (Pole 1991) which was intended to aid record keeping and prove useful during up-date sessions. However, not all members of staff or pupils were completely at ease with the computer; and in spite of its use, the process relied, to a great extent, on the passing of paper between members of staff.

Although the Record of Achievement which was agreed between teacher and pupils was based on comments from all the staff with whom the pupil had contact, there was no provision within the system for formal discussion between staff about individual pupils. The form tutor was in most cases, therefore, negotiating and discussing with pupils on the basis of ticks in boxes from subject teachers, without comment or explanation. In this respect the passing of paper between staff was a crucial factor in keeping the Record of Achievement process moving. The Record of Achievement co-ordinator explained that an important part of her job was 'chasing people up' to ensure the process ran smoothly, and that members of staff adhered to the timetable which she devised at the beginning of each year. She gave the following example as a typical 'chase up' activity in which she was involved:

> All our kids are setted for nearly all subjects . . . so it's difficult to know which teachers haven't done their Geography for example, because you might have three people teaching Geography. So this time I've done a sheet . . . Descriptors should be in [to form tutors] by Monday at 3.30 pm, and then I put a sheet out and say 'have you got all your descriptors in, and if not will you let me know?' And they have to check through, and they want me to do any chasing up. Really it's just the odd one or two.

In order to conduct a successful negotiation session form tutors must have the descriptors completed by the subject teachers. Without these, they were unable to discuss with pupils the particular skills, experiences and abilities specified on the descriptor sheets. The development of the Record of Achievement in such a way placed a primacy on keeping the process going, and the co-ordinator had a central role in keeping the paper moving.

In most cases, subject teachers were also form tutors. This meant that most members of staff were 'users' as well as 'providers' of completed descriptor sheets. Furthermore, where form tutors taught members of their tutor group for a particular lesson, which given the size of Benton School was by no means uncommon, the process required that they complete descriptor sheets which they would then use themselves, in the negotiation sessions. Whilst such a process may be seen as unnecessarily bureaucratic, it ensured that each negotiation session was based on the same amount and style of formal information. George James, a Chemistry teacher, who expressed a considerable degree of scepticism over the entire Records of Achievement process and philosophy explained his approach to this situation.

> To save time early on I used to not do some profiles because I used to have to hand them in to myself. You know what I mean. I'd do them and I get them back. And I say 'look Ooh yes it's from me', so I didn't bother doing it.

However, as George explained by actually completing the descriptor sheet for pupils in his own tutor group he was able to put into perspective their performance in other areas of the curriculum, and to form a more comprehensive view of the pupils. He continued:

> This year I actually did that [completed descriptor sheets for his own tutor group] just to see, because your judgement is often coloured by what you see on paper in front of you. I did that just to see how mine came out against everybody else's. And they were just about the same.

The Record of Achievement process appeared to have provided George with a more holistic view of his personal tutees, which might otherwise have been denied him had he only been aware of their achievements in his Chemistry lessons. It enabled him to view his pupils' performance in Chemistry in relation to all other subjects on the timetable.

The small turnover of staff in the school meant that most had become familiar with the process as it had evolved and had taken a hand in shaping it. Several teachers claimed to have made suggestions which resulted in streamlining the process. For example, concern had been expressed over the amount of paper generated by the process. This made the procedures cumbersome and expensive in terms of paper and photocopying. Jackie Saunders, the Record of Achievement Co-ordinator, explained how the amount of paper used was cut down.

> One thing I instigated at the suggestion of the CDT chappies which was quite a good idea, and certainly it saves paper. Instead of everyone having one of these sheets [main descriptor sheet for each pupil] we just have one master sheet each and we have strips of paper with boxes, and just line it up.

The change meant that rather than several lists being produced for each discussion session, one master list of descriptors could be used for all the sessions. Whilst only a small modification to the whole process, it was nevertheless important in engendering a sense of ownership and influence by the staff.

Although the Warwickshire Record of Achievement varied between schools, as heads and staff were given latitude to adapt the process and documents to fit the particular needs of their own school, the general approach remained broadly similar throughout the areas of the LEA where Records of Achievement were promoted. The process relied on effective communication between teachers and pupils, it required an identification of strengths and weaknesses of the pupils to facilitate development and to build on their achievements. The process also required effective administration with commitment from teachers and pupils.

Given these prerequisites a series of questions emerged which were concerned not only with the Record of Achievement itself but also with its effect on a wide range of issues relating to teaching, learning and the management of education. For example, did the need for honest dialogue and 'negotiation' between teacher and pupil challenge the traditional role of the teacher which relies on the teacher being viewed as the figure of authority? Did the fact that Records of Achievement in Benton School required on-going formative assessment necessitate changes in teaching style? What was the reaction of parents to the new reporting strategies? What demands did Records of Achievement make of teachers and pupils? Had Records of Achievement become integrated with the everyday activities of the school? In what way did they contribute to the development of the pupil?

The diversity of issues and questions highlighted by the introduction and development of Records of Achievement demonstrate the potential which they have as a catalyst for change in schools. The questions outlined above provided important guidance for this research. Having provided the background to this study and outlined the Record of Achievement process, the discussion which follows will address these and similar questions.

2

FITTING IT ALL IN: IT'S A QUESTION OF TIME

By the time that this research was conducted (during the academic year 1989–90) Records of Achievement were well established in Benton, the school having been used as an original LEA pilot for the scheme some five years beforehand. A generation of pupils had, therefore, moved through the school for whom this kind of reporting and recording of procedure was the norm.

Similarly, for some staff the Record of Achievement process was now an integral part of their duties. For others, however, the process still posed a challenge largely in terms of the time taken to complete descriptor sheets for all their pupils, and to conduct effective one-to-one negotiation or discussion sessions. Opposition, largely on the grounds of time, had been greater when the scheme had first been introduced to the school.

Nevertheless, the commitment of the head and the deputy to the philosophy of Records of Achievement, together with the status and attention which the school received during the period in which it piloted Records of Achievement for the LEA, provided a great boost to their development and take-up. Pete Robbins, the deputy, recalled however, that not all members of staff were totally committed to the idea from the outset:

> I mean to be honest . . . only half the staff were for it. Now
> to persuade some of them, the main bugbear they saw was
> time. Now we convinced them I believe because we said to
> start with you won't have to do reports, because Records of
> Achievement were going to replace reports.

To gain the confidence and co-operation of the more sceptical
members of staff, Records of Achievement were presented in terms
of a trade-off with traditional reports. Pete Robbins recalled that
although this was successful with some staff, others thought that the
decision to dispense with traditional reports was in itself a retrograde step. At this early stage, however, the traditional report acted
as a bargaining point for the more reluctant staff. Nevertheless,
gaining the support of all was difficult (cf. Mansell (1984) on the
status of profiles). Again Pete Robbins remembered the early
developments of Records of Achievement:

> I think initially it was more work, it took quite a lot of selling.

Until procedures were worked out and streamlined the Record of
Achievement process required a considerable investment of time
from staff, which some resented. Eventually, Pete Robbins believes
that many staff were convinced of the value of Records of Achievement when they saw what could be achieved with pupils, quite
simply during the negotiation sessions. He continued:

> I think once you've got a member of staff into the negotiation
> room they can actually see the benefits.

Undoubtedly, most members of staff agreed that there were considerable benefits to be derived from engaging in individual discussions with pupils and in this sense agreed with the sentiments
expressed by the deputy head. Yet in spite of the fact that Records
of Achievement were long established in the school and formed part
of a whole-school policy on reporting and recording, the question
of time remained fundamentally important.

Questions of time relate not only to the length of time necessary
to see through the Record of Achievement process successfully, but
also to the quality of assessment and reporting facilitated by the
process. As we have seen, the time taken for Records of Achievement was frequently compared with the time required to complete
traditional school reports. There was little doubt that Records of

Achievement demanded not only more time, but more time over a longer period of the school year, than reports ever did. For example, teachers were required to complete a descriptor list for each pupil they taught in relation to their different subject specialisms and to conduct a one-to-one discussion with each member of their tutor group. In many cases where teachers taught more than one subject they would complete more than one set of descriptors for the individual pupils with whom they had contact. They may, for example, spend 6–10 minutes per pupil in each of their English classes, the same for their Geography classes and so on. In addition, most staff would have approximately 25 personal tutees with whom to conduct an individual discussion.

Clearly, the more subjects a teacher taught, the more time would be required. The fact that Benton School had only a small staff meant that all teachers had responsibility for more than one subject. With average teaching groups of 25 pupils, time required to complete the records was, therefore, considerable. The head fully recognized this. In assessing the overall state of Records of Achievement in the school he said:

> I'm really very pleased with the way it's going, I mean it is more time consuming, and higher on the agenda than school reports have ever been, and it's always there.

Whilst the comparisons with the traditional reports were used as a trade-off for the introduction of Records of Achievement, direct comparisons between the two are surely erroneous. To see the Record of Achievement merely as a glorified report is to ignore many of the developmental qualities which it embodies. Nevertheless, such a comparison was used in Benton School.

Although most staff shared the head's view on the increased time commitment for Records of Achievement, the fact that they did consume so much time meant that not all staff shared his enthusiasm. For example, several teachers who had experience, both of Records of Achievement and traditional reports, had reservations about the amount of time required and the pay-off in terms of the level of detail which they provide. One teacher drew particular attention to this issue in relation to providing information to parents. His scepticism of the whole Record of Achievement process came to light during a conversation about experiences at parents' evenings. He explained:

Put it like this, last night's parents' evening for fifth years . . .
There's no way they can find out how their kids have done in
mock exam results. So I did a little piece of paper for them, and
at least three of them said thank you very much. Where do they
get it? They don't get information like that from Records of
Achievement you see.

The teacher's concern was based on a belief that using the Record
of Achievement as the principal means of communicating with
parents was inadequate.

Not only did he have reservations about the amount of time
required for Records of Achievement, but he also felt that in spite
of this they failed to provide parents with important information
about the progress of their children in specific subject areas. He was
not alone in his criticisms. Alan Neville, again a teacher with experience of Records of Achievement and traditional reports, went further in his criticisms. In a discussion about the amount of time spent
on Records of Achievement and their value, he summed up the
process as follows:

I would say with the second and third years it's a waste of time.
And the fourth and fifth years it's worth having, well fifth
years particularly, but possibly the fourth years to lead in to
the fifth year. I don't think you need second and third years,
to train them how to do it so that when they get to fourth and
fifth years they know all about it.

Whilst Alan Neville counted himself generally as a supporter of
Records of Achievement, he identified their strength almost entirely
in terms of the summative document and its capacity to contribute to employers' knowledge of potential recruits. Consequently he
regarded time spent on the Record of Achievement process during
the second and third year as time that could be best spent on other
activities.

In theory, all Benton staff involved in one-to-one pupil discussions received one non-teaching period per week during which they
were to be conducted. In practice, however, this period had been
taken from their existing allocation of non-teaching time. Not sur-
prisingly there was considerable disquiet about this with some staff
feeling that they had lost out on preparation and marking time at the
expense of the Record of Achievement.

Concern over the time taken for Records of Achievement was expressed even by their most fervent supporters. Concern related not to fear of, or being unwilling to engage in any of the extra work entailed, but to pressure it placed on other areas of schooling. Jane Upton, a third-year tutor, expressed her worries over pressure and time in these terms:

> I think at the moment there is too much. People are tired and I think you can quite easily get yourself into a situation whereby the cost is so much, the work gone into it, you leave other work, and then you catch up with other work, and then you're leaving this and it all piles up.

The problem she described clearly was not caused by Records of Achievement alone, but by the accumulation of responsibilities, other new initiatives and extra-curricular activities, in addition to teaching duties. In this scenario it is important to identify Records of Achievement as just one of the many activities in schools, all of which require time and commitment, and act to place pressure on the classroom teacher.

Jane Upton voiced these concerns as we continued our discussion of time and the importance attached to Records of Achievement in Benton School. She believed the pressure on time may have contributed to severe ill feeling amongst staff towards Records of Achievement. She explained:

> . . . So you have given up all the time that you would be using to do other work. And I think sometimes they have built up a bit of resentment. I think that the basic problem here at the moment, [is that] two years ago it was just Records of Achievement that we were dealing with, we are now dealing with three or four other little babies at the same time, and the staff are getting very very tired and very very irritated.

Furthermore, it would seem that where lack of time adds pressure the quality of staff input to Records of Achievement and other initiatives suffers. Jane Upton had had experience of this:

> I think that they [the staff] are rushing into a lot of things. I rushed into one of these [negotiation sessions] the other day and I felt bad about it afterwards.

Timetables and constraints

The Record of Achievement process required staff to adhere to a fairly tight timetable in terms of completion of documentation and more specifically the one-to-one pupil negotiations. As negotiations were scheduled to take place in the room specially designated as the 'negotiation room', it was imperative that tutors kept up to date with their negotiations. Slippage on these put the timetable for use of the negotiation room at risk. This has implications for the whole programme. Consequently, staff felt a pressure to keep up to date and in some cases there was a feeling of a need to get negotiations over and done with. Jackie Saunders expressed such a view:

> Now I get two hours [free periods/negotiation time] on a Monday which seems a good opportunity to get as many done as possible, and I try and do four if I can, on Monday. Once I'm in the mood I'd rather do it you know, get it out of the way.

Rather than merely dismissing the negotiation sessions as something to get out of the way, other members of staff saw them, and the process of completing descriptor sheets as making an important contribution to their relationship with the pupil and their understanding of them. Janet Fitch, one of the younger members of staff, explained why she considered time for Records of Achievement to be time well spent. She said:

> It's very time consuming and I don't think any one of us here would disagree with that, and to be faced with often 30 or more descriptors to fill in, debate over, and think about is time consuming. But by the same token, I think by doing the actual process of it, it's almost as therapeutic for yourself as it is for the child, even when you're filling it in because you're thinking exclusively about that individual.

Clearly, for this teacher the time required for the Record of Achievement process was adequately compensated for by their contribution to her knowledge and understanding of the pupils. Consequently, the time taken was not seen in any way as a burden, but rather as a means by which teacher–pupil relationships may be enhanced, and as an opportunity for the teacher to discover more about the pupil as an individual rather than a member of a larger group.

Furthermore, to put this half an hour discussion in perspective, it could be the only time in an entire year of schooling that the pupils could guarantee the attention of a member of staff on their own. Or to take this even further, in some schools where discussion in the context of Records of Achievement occurred only in the fourth or fifth year, the half an hour interview could be the only time during 11 years of compulsory schooling that a pupil engaged in a one-to-one exchange with a teacher for a length of time longer than a few minutes and for reasons other than those relating to discipline. Clearly, speculation of this nature is to adopt the worst possible case, but it serves to illustrate the point that whilst the Record of Achievement discussion sessions may prove to be particularly time consuming for members of staff, they may represent a rare opportunity for pupils to engage in discussion about their achievements and progress. Given that the process is designed to be of principal benefit to pupils rather than teachers it may be useful to keep the worst-case scenario in mind.

Time taken for one-to-one negotiation sessions between teachers and pupils in Benton School tended to vary considerably according to the teacher and pupil concerned. Each session was officially scheduled to last 30 minutes, and staff had the appropriate amount of time allocated to them for the use of the negotiation room where the sessions were to take place. Teachers were required to keep to half an hour sessions in order that the process should run smoothly and each member of staff have access to the negotiation room in the order and times at which they were scheduled for it. However, conversations with staff revealed that pressure was often imposed on the process by the need to adhere to the negotiation-room timetable. For example, more than one teacher recalled a time when their negotiation session had taken longer than the allotted half an hour. Owing to another member of staff waiting to use the room, the session was brought hurriedly to an end. Janet Fitch, who had experienced such a situation, explained that she was now reluctant to use the negotiation room because of the prohibitive time constraint it placed on the sessions. There was, however, nowhere else in the school which offered the same degree of privacy. Consequently she continued to use the negotiation room.

In general it appeared that most staff did complete their negotiation sessions within the half hour and whilst sessions could take much longer they had to be moulded or geared to fit into the time allocated. The practical reasons for this are obvious but the application of a time constraint, either overtly or covertly, would seem to run counter to the Records of Achievement philosophy of free and open discussions between teacher and pupil. However, an interview with Michael Anderson, a fourth-year tutor, revealed the reality of the situation with regard to the time required to negotiate with a complete tutor group.

CP: How long does a negotiation session last roughly?

MA: A quick one would be about half an hour, and a slow one could take an hour. It just depends how much agreement there is initially. If on every prompt you have disagreement then it can go on for an awful long time.

CP: So that can take up quite a lot of time. How many have you got in your form?

MA: I have a form of 24 at the moment. So the actual negotiation could be either 12 hours or 24 hours depending on how it goes and then in addition to that you've got all the collating and gathering of information.

From Michael Anderson's account of the negotiation sessions two issues are apparent. Firstly, it would seem that negotiation sessions are unpredictable in content and in the extent to which teachers and pupils agree over the topics under discussion. Consequently, allocating a specific time period to the sessions or keeping to a rigid timetable was difficult. Quite often teachers and pupils were kept waiting for their turn in the negotiation room. Secondly, Michael Anderson implied that agreement between teacher and pupil reduced the need for discussion and so made negotiation sessions shorter. Interviews with several fifth-year pupils during the course of this research corroborated this.

For example, Paul, John and Sally, three fifth-year pupils with three years' experience of negotiations in the Record of Achievement process, gave examples of how long sessions have taken for them.

CP: What about negotiation sessions, how long do they usually take?

John: It depends how many you agree on. Once I'd agreed on nearly everything and it was over in ten minutes.

CP: What about you Paul, what would you say?

Paul: Yes, I usually agree on everything and we just go straight through.

CP: And you Sally?

Sally: About ten minutes.

In each case, these three fifth years from the high-ability group had experienced very short and apparently straightforward negotiation sessions. The implication behind the examples they gave and that of Michael Anderson is that if agreement over each descriptor was reached without great difficulty, then little discussion of the issues addressed by the descriptors appeared to take place. In such cases it would seem that negotiation which was regarded as central to the Record of Achievement process was bypassed, being reduced to little more than a routine administrative task, carried out as quickly as possible by the parties involved. Where teachers were pressed for time it could be that there was a temptation to skip through the descriptors quickly, thereby reducing the time required for discussion. This may have been achieved by teachers agreeing with the views of the pupils or alternatively, the pupils were encouraged to accept their teachers' views of them with little negotiation. Either way, discussion could be very limited.

It should not be inferred, however, that all negotiation sessions were straightforward, taking only a matter of ten minutes. It has already been shown, for example, that for Michael Anderson a short negotiation session was usually in the region of half an hour. Furthermore, pupil interviews brought to light many instances where sessions took up to, and in some cases beyond, an hour. Charlotte, a fifth-year girl, again from the high-ability group, described one of her recent negotiation sessions with her form tutor Mr Shaw, thus:

Charlotte: I won't say something for the sake of it, and if Mr Shaw is trying to con me into accepting one [a descriptor] that I don't agree with then I won't agree with him. Then we'll have a big discussion [Charlotte gesticulates to indicate big discussion should be in inverted commas] about it.

CP: Big discussions in inverted commas, why in inverted commas?

Charlotte: Because Mr Shaw tends to get a bit narky if you don't agree with him.

In this case the failure to agree meant the negotiation time was prolonged considerably until what Charlotte describes as a 'rational conclusion' was reached. In this instance the need to discuss many issues on which teacher and pupil could not initially agree was probably enhanced by the particularly vociferous and articulate character of the fifth-year pupil, who admitted to enjoying negotiation sessions and the opportunity they provided to discuss her own achievements. Charlotte openly admitted to enjoying the attention that negotiation brought to her. She stated:

> I love doing that [talking about her achievements and out of school activities] because I love telling people about myself.

It would appear in this case that the ebullient personality of the pupil contributed to her involvement in the negotiation process, and consequently to the length of the session. Again this would seem to present difficulties in terms of operating a rigid timetable for discussion.

Louise, a fifth year in the same group and again very articulate, described a similar negotiation experience with Mr Shaw:

> *Louise*: I used to do all the talking, but this one took one hour and ten minutes and I missed my bus, so now I've quietened down a bit, so that I don't miss the bus.
>
> *CP*: An hour and ten minutes, that's quite a long time isn't it?
>
> *Louise*: Yeah, we were only allocated 30 minutes but Mr Shaw sort of got me talking and I got talking myself and that was it.

Although with both Louise and Charlotte, conversation with Mr Shaw flowed easily during the negotiation sessions and there was clearly a great deal to discuss, there was still an expectation that all of this should take no longer than half an hour. Louise and Charlotte made this point:

> *Charlotte*: No one ever takes less than 30 minutes. It never runs to time.
>
> *CP*: Do you have to keep it to 30 minutes?
>
> *Louise*: I feel there is pressure to now because I got the mick taken out of me for being so long.

CP: Why did you get the mick taken out of you then?
Louise: I don't know, just for being a chatterbox.

Interestingly, in these two cases, where the negotiation sessions had clearly proved to be most successful, pupils identified pressure to complete the sessions in shorter time. Furthermore, the fact that Louise's one hour and ten minute session had become common knowledge with pupils and staff throughout the school would seem to imply that negotiation which was allowed to take so long was out of the ordinary and perhaps too long. Given the centrality of the negotiation session to the whole Record of Achievement process in Benton School, the emphasis placed on its contribution to improved teacher–pupil relationships, and the objective of enhanced communication and social skills, such implications are surely unwarranted.

One third-year tutor with a strong belief that the negotiation sessions have a great deal to offer pupils resisted pressure to cut down the time taken for negotiation sessions. He explained:

Tutor: . . . it's very time consuming this negotiation routine, it takes a lot of time to get it organized, you know, I sit with one pupil every week on a Wednesday, it takes me a full hour, if I want to do it properly.
CP: Are these fourth years?
Tutor: Third years. You know, if I want to do it properly and I want to get everything across to that particular pupil, you know, to make him understood what he's got to do, or she's got to do, you know it will take an hour. And if I had more time, you know, maybe it would take more than an hour.
CP: Is there often pressure to get them into half an hour?
Tutor: Well, you know, because I take an hour, a lot of other members of staff say they can do two in an hour, maybe three in an hour. You know, I've fallen behind, but I feel, you know, the ones that I have done, they've been done, really thoroughly, and the pupil has got a sense of achievement from them, he's got a great deal out of the negotiation, he's been put on the right track sort of thing.

In this instance the tutor saw the negotiation session in terms of him informing the pupil of what he or she had 'got to do'. It would seem, therefore, that the capacity for negotiation can be limited by the tutor's perception of the session in terms of making the pupil understand what he or she has to do. Rather than a situation of balance, the negotiation session in this instance may be seen in terms of the tutor seeking to exert or substantiate control over the pupil. If this is indeed the case then there would seem to be some contradiction between the practice of discussion and the Record of Achievement philosophy which seeks a situation of greater equality and reciprocity between teacher and pupil. In this teacher's experience, the discussion session was an opportunity to put pupils 'on the right track' and it was the time required to achieve this rather than any open exchange between teacher and pupil which drove the process.

The fact that such variations in the time taken for negotiation sessions have been cited by pupils and staff illustrates the difficulties of running the sessions according to a strict timetable. In several cases it would appear that it was the availability of the designated negotiation room which imposed time constraints on the sessions, rather than issues intrinsic to the process, and in others the personality of the pupils seemed to enhance the discussion sessions. These few examples from Benton School illustrate the human dimension of the Record of Achievement process. They demonstrate that as with all human interaction things are unpredictable. The fact that the process rests essentially on discussion and that discussion is mediated by a wide variety of social variables, means that the imposition of a timetable is likely to render the whole process artificial. In this case it would seem that the application of structure to an activity which in the Records of Achievement context is intended to be wide ranging and comprehensive is to seriously limit the benefit which pupils and teachers might derive from the whole process.

Time required for the Record of Achievement process was an issue not only for staff but also for the Benton pupil. In particular pupils were required to give time to the completion of descriptor sheets prior to the discussion session with their tutor. The importance of the sheets was stressed to the pupils by the staff and the head, and they were encouraged to take the process seriously, to consider the different statements carefully before ticking the appropriate boxes. However, interviews with the pupils revealed that this was not always the case. Whilst some estimated that completion of the descriptor sheets took approximately half an hour, others quoted much shorter periods of time, and even admitted to completing the forms during a short bus journey to school. Moreover, two fifth-year girls explained that by the time they got to the fifth year they no longer needed to spend such a long time considering the descriptors. The following excerpt from our interview illustrated this point.

CP: You know when you take your descriptor sheets home, how long do you take to fill them in?

Susan: Five minutes [laughter]. You don't tend to change a lot in like nine months.

CP: So you don't take very long then to fill them in?

Julie: No. You won't tell anybody will you?

These pupils were familiar with the descriptors from the previous year, as fourth- and fifth-year descriptors were the same, and with the process from their first year in the school. For these pupils and many of their peers, the act of completing the descriptor sheets took little time, and consequently involved little contemplation or reviewing of their achievements and development from the fourth to the fifth year.

It would seem from this that the formative Record of Achievement process involved an intrinsic learning process. The more familiar pupils became with the descriptors, the quicker the process became. This again reduced the time spent on serious consideration and reflection on the various descriptors. For members of staff, however, completion of descriptor sheets was often very time consuming. Where they had teaching responsibilities for several different subjects which resulted in contact with a greater number of pupils the number of descriptor sheets which they were required to complete was substantial. For example, we have already seen that Susan Watts taught History, Social Science, English and Special Needs. She was required to complete descriptors for pupils in all of these groups. During an interview she discussed some of the difficulties that this presented.

CP: So when you come to do them then [i.e. complete the descriptor sheets] in very basic terms, are you able to put a face to every name?

SW: The only problem that I do have is, [pause] yes, I can definitely put a face to every Record of Achievement that I fill in. I wouldn't fill one in if I couldn't . . . there are one or two quiet little girls that I need to put a face to before I start to comment.

Although all teachers assured me that they could always put a face to a name before completing descriptor sheets, in some cases the impression gained was that their knowledge of the individual pupil ended there, and perhaps the process acted against the 'quiet little girls'. If this was the case, then the degree to which staff were able to make informed comments and judgements about the pupils must surely be questioned. In this context the tick-box format of the descriptor sheets gave little indication of how well the teacher knew the individual pupil. The need to keep the process moving and keep to schedule, may have meant that teachers were forced to complete descriptor sheets before getting to know their pupils in any detail.

Timing of the process

Discussion in this chapter thus far has focused on the time required to complete the Record of Achievement process. An issue allied to this, however, relates to the timing of the individual teacher–pupil negotiation or discussion sessions. Whilst the philosophy of Records of Achievement (Garforth and Macintosh 1986; Hitchcock 1986a; Broadfoot 1987) stresses the formative importance of the process of reviewing and recording progress, an intrinsic assumption in this philosophy is that the process is ongoing. Within Benton School the intention has clearly been to encourage a reflexive approach to reporting and recording amongst both staff and pupils. Nevertheless, the fact that only one discussion session was scheduled for each academic year, meant a decision had to be taken as to when this should take place.

Within Benton School the options for the negotiation sessions were identified in terms of a rolling programme throughout the year, or a block of time devoted solely to negotiations for all pupils or particular year groups of pupils at a specified point in the school year. In discussion with the headteacher, pros and cons of each option were pointed out. With the rolling programme difficulties existed in relation to different pupils engaging in discussion sessions at quite different times of the school year. For example, in a tutor group of 28 several pupils may have a discussion session near the start of the Autumn term, several towards the start of the Summer term and the majority in between. Problems arose with the early negotiations in that there may have been little to discuss or progress shown, given their proximity to the beginning of the school year. With those closer to the end of the year, however, concern was expressed by some staff that this left insufficient time for fifth years to use their final Record of Achievement as an aid in the job finding process.

Despite these shortcomings, the rolling programme had been adopted by Benton School for a number of reasons and after trying a system of blocking discussion sessions at particular times during the year. The head explained the decision to change the arrangements in the following terms:

> One of the reasons why it's [the Record of Achievement process] high on the agenda is that it never actually goes away.

By introducing a rolling programme staff and students were constantly aware of the Record of Achievement. The head believed that this encouraged staff to view pupil achievement holistically and to integrate the practice of recording and reviewing with everyday classroom activities. He continued:

> It's higher on the agenda now we've got a rolling programme than ever it was when we just had a three-day slot, where a tutor negotiated the group over a three-day period. Then it was Records of Achievement week. Now we've got a rolling programme it never goes away.

The decision to move towards a rolling programme relates directly to the head's intention that by becoming integrated with everyday activities, the Record of Achievement should cease to be regarded as something special. Rather, it would become ordinary and encourage pupils to take responsibility for parts of their own learning by putting the emphasis on them to recognize their strengths and weaknesses and to take appropriate actions to enhance achievement. Without this approach, the head feared that Records of Achievement could become ghettoized. He described the school's previous attempts at blocking negotiations for year groups in the following terms:

> All the third years, for example, would be prepared and the paperwork would be done for them. There would be a three-day slot and supply teachers and the form tutors would negotiate the whole group . . . but you tended to get the feeling that, well, this is the Record of Achievement slot in this year.

Not only did such an approach act to isolate the discussion process from the rest of the year's activities, it also necessitated the employment of supply teachers, which was a financial cost to the school and meant disruption of lessons for those pupils who would normally have been taught by those staff involved in the negotiation sessions. In addition, the head identified another difficulty in relation to the blocking of negotiation. He continued:

> Plus with that sort of negotiation, the third day the pupils get a very raw deal. However good the negotiator they get a very raw deal.

Other members of staff also referred to what might be termed 'negotiation burnout' which meant they were unable to give all pupils equal attention during the negotiation block. Overall, the experience of the block negotiation encouraged the Benton head and staff to develop the rolling programme, to recognize its limitations and to seek to work around them. This had the effect of keeping Records of Achievement in people's minds throughout the year. Again the headteacher explained:

> . . . it's in front all the time. You're either preparing, negotiating or updating someone all through the year.

From observations conducted in the school throughout the Spring term, it would seem that the head had achieved his objective of keeping the Record of Achievement process high on the agenda. Negotiations were ongoing and Records of Achievement, like many other common school practices, were a constant source of conversation in the staffroom.

Integration

Underpinning this whole debate about time required for Records of Achievement and the timing of teacher–pupil discussion sessions is the wider issue of the extent to which the Record of Achievement process is integrated with the fundamental activities of teaching and learning and the extent to which it forms part of the pupils' experience of schooling.

The DES (1984) statement of policy made clear that Records of Achievement are to be a central tenet of the curriculum, teaching and organization:

> The recording process should help schools to identify the all-round potential of their pupils and to consider how well their curriculum, teaching and organization enable pupils to develop the general practical and social skills which are to be recorded.

To have such an impact the Record of Achievement process must surely be much more than an additional extra. In this sense an interpretation which sees Records of Achievement as taking time away from essential activities of teaching and learning is to misunderstand the importance which has been attached to it. If such importance is attached to the Record of Achievement, which some commentators believe should be the case (cf. Evans 1988; Hall 1989; Munby 1989) then concern about time required for them is unwarranted. If, as would seem to be the wish of some practitioners and educational researchers (Stansbury 1985; Hicks 1986; Hitchcock 1986a) Records of Achievement become fully integrated with school curriculum and organization, then debates about time required for them may be applied equally to such activities as school assemblies, tests, sports days and even timetabled lessons.

The experiences of the teachers and pupils described in this chapter have demonstrated that time is a critical issue in the Record of Achievement process. Furthermore, they have demonstrated some of the complexities of the matter. For example, whilst it may be tempting to assert that the Record of Achievement process could be improved with the allocation of more time to it, this would surely be to over-simplify the problems. The evidence suggests that some of the difficulties relating to time were intrinsic to the process established in Benton School. For example, the need to adhere to a rigid timetable for the use of a specific room in which to conduct negotiations placed artificial constraints on the discussion process. In addition, the reliance on descriptor sheets seemed at the same time to bureaucratize the process of teacher–pupil interaction and to provide a means of moving quickly through the process to the detriment of real discussion.

Underpinning all of this it must also be borne in mind that Records of Achievement are just one of the many things on the school agenda which compete for the time and attention of teachers and pupils.

3

BATTERING DOWN AND MIDDLING OUT: PUPIL-TEACHER DISCUSSIONS

The importance of pupil–teacher discussion has already been identified as central to the Record of Achievement process and some of
the implications in relation to time for discussion or negotiation
have been outlined. This chapter examines the interaction of
teacher–pupil discussion and considers staff and student views and
experiences.

In Benton School, teacher–pupil discussion was referred to as
negotiation. Negotiation was a highly structured event which took
place at a specified time and in a particular room in the school.
The negotiation was, in many respects, regarded as the most important aspect of the Record of Achievement process, prior to which
considerable preparation by staff and students was carried out to
facilitate effective discussion. The deputy head was in no doubt
about the benefits which could be derived from the negotiation
session. He commented in the following terms:

> Once you've got a member of staff into the negotiation room
> they can actually see the benefits. I mean, I went into the
> negotiation room for half an hour, and I had half an hour just
> talking and listening, and it's amazing, really amazing.

For many Benton staff, the negotiation session provided an opportunity to get to know their pupils as individuals. On several occasions during interviews for this research, staff recalled learning things about pupils during negotiation sessions which had not and probably would not have come to light during other kinds of contact. These may have been things to do with hobbies or achievements outside the school setting or more sensitive issues concerning relationships and family matters. For example, during a negotiation session one pupil discussed her difficulties in communicating with her father. Her teacher believed that as a result the pupil became determined to confront the difficulty and relations between father and daughter improved. The intimacy of the negotiation session allowed conversations of that nature and the promise of confidentiality was also intended to enhance the feeling of trust between teacher and pupil.

One of the principal roles of the negotiation session would seem, therefore, to be in providing some kind of pastoral support for those pupils who needed it. This was clearly identified by members of staff, some of whom had used the negotiation sessions as a first step towards helping pupils to make contact with other support agencies, as an effective use of the allotted discussion time. Nevertheless, discussion of a pastoral nature occurred as part of the negotiation or discussion session and in this respect was structured by the constraints of the location, time and the intended outcome of the process. Whilst teachers and some pupils saw the negotiation sessions as contributing to pastoral support in the school it is important to see the pastoral discussions which occurred in this context as part of the formal structure of the Record of Achievement process and as such they were constrained by it. The strength of such discussions rested in their capacity to alert staff to particular issues which could be pursued, if necessary, outside the Record of Achievement context. Several Benton teachers were convinced that without the structure which the negotiation session offered, some pupils would have been reluctant to bring pastoral issues to the attention of the staff. The structure operated, therefore, as a means of legitimation for discussion of a wide range of issues which was perhaps not provided at other times in the school.

In the main, however, negotiation sessions were the principal opportunity for staff and pupils to review progress to talk about strengths and weaknesses and to identify means by which pupils could enhance their performance at school. This function of the negotiation session was seen to be relevant to all pupils (Burgess and Adams 1985) in Benton School regardless of ability or the extent of their achievements. In this sense, the Benton philosophy of Records of Achievement was well removed from that of Sir Keith Joseph's who originally saw them as a means of formally documenting the achievements of the less able (Broadfoot 1986). The Benton head extolled this philosophy in the following terms:

> I don't think there are any children too bright to benefit. Because you are academically able doesn't make you socially competent or give you personal skills . . . (high academic ability) doesn't stop us trying to identify areas of strength and weakness . . . I would have thought to continue to talk to children like that on a one-to-one basis is the key to get them to think about what they are doing [and] can only be of positive help.

The notion of all pupils thinking about their performance in school activities, reviewing their achievements and identifying means of enhancing levels of accomplishment which the head introduced here is really the key to the negotiation process. In many respects the whole Record of Achievement process was designed to facilitate self-review and reflection on the part of the pupils. To this end the structured programme of review based around the pre-specified descriptors (Appendix 1) was designed to cover the whole range of school activities, together with out-of-school activities which related to leisure time and to the home. In addition, a section was also included on attitudes and social qualities. The intention was, therefore, that by talking through this wide range of issues pupils would come to identify the areas, not only in their school performance but also in their general social development, which required greater effort or more attention. Or by talking about achievement and accomplishment it was hoped that pupils would recognize the need to consolidate effort in particular areas. The discussion should, therefore, act to motivate pupils and to help them to take responsibility for their own development, not only in relation to the specific issues which were discussed during the session, but in relation to their education and life more generally.

In the context of the negotiation session, therefore, the teacher adopted a position of neutrality, he or she was there in the role of facilitator seeking to help the pupil to see ways in which, not only school, but also life performance could be enhanced. The neutrality of the teacher in this role meant that he or she did not judge the negotiation performance of the pupil but sought to use it to the advantage of the pupil. However, to suggest that the teacher is neutral in this context is perhaps to assume that the teacher was able to distance himself or herself from the traditional role of assessor. Hargreaves and colleagues (1988) suggest that pupils may perceive the negotiation as an opportunity to demonstrate verbal dexterity, all round accomplishments and even negotiation skills *per se*. If this proves to be the case then it seems likely that teachers' perceptions of pupil performance at negotiation may come to influence the judgements they make of them in terms of ability, motivation, etc. In short, rather than a neutral situation, the negotiation session may become another opportunity for teachers to assess pupils, not in terms of their achievements over the preceding school year, but in terms of how they 'perform' during negotiation sessions.

Furthermore, by collecting information about out-of-school activities, social and personal qualities, in addition to school based achievements, the teacher has the potential to judge the pupil socially as well as academically. According to Hargreaves *et al.* (1988: 135) this potential for holistic assessment may result in an approach which:

> . . . treats personal and social development not as something peripheral to or isolated from the rest of the schools' curriculum and organization, but as something that is absolutely central to the entire educational process; something that is inextricably intertwined with curriculum, organization, teaching style and assessment.

Whilst one might see the potential for such an approach in raising the status of personal and social education in schools there are also inherent dangers. For example, the complete integration of personal and social development with the school curriculum and organization may again lead to temptations to assess personal and social qualities in the same way as one might assess reading or mathematical ability.

In some ways the Benton Record of Achievement already did this. For example, Section 1 of the descriptor list (Appendix 1) was headed 'Personal and Social Qualities'. Under this heading teacher and pupil were required to make judgements in relation to 'cheerfulness', 'open mindedness', 'self-assurance', 'sociability', and other such qualities. Under the heading 'sociability' for instance, teacher and pupil were required to make a judgement of the latter's relationships with family and friends by choosing one of the following statements:

9.0 Sociability
9.1 A popular and central figure with a wide circle of friends.
9.2 Forms and maintains good relationships with fellow pupils and adults.
9.3 Whilst getting on well with a small group of friends he/she finds it difficult to form relationships with other people.
9.4 Is able to mix well with fellow pupils but prefers to be alone.
9.5 Relationships with others can be spoilt by a lack of self-restraint.
9.6 Has only one or two friends.
9.7 Has great difficulty in relating to anyone outside the immediate family.

In this instance what may be very personal issues are subject to the same kind of assessment and judgements as the pupils' performance in school subjects or the Duke of Edinburgh's Award Scheme. There would seem to be a fundamental confusion here between qualities and abilities or achievements. Furthermore, the confusion rests not only on whether it is indeed possible to assess qualities, but also on whether it is ethically desirable. Attempts to assess pupils' social qualities must by definition imply that it is possible to judge qualities against a set of standards. The question arises, therefore, as to whose standards these are and what values are implicit within them. Bridges (1989: 122) takes up this issue in the context of aspirations to report on the whole child. He says:

> . . . any aspiration to report on 'the whole child' carries the implication of a prescription of what counts as, or what ought to constitute, that whole child. Any such prescription ought properly to be accompanied by some explanation and defence of the values and/or social context which it assumes.

Whilst it would be unfair to assert that Benton pupils' personal and social qualities were being compared against an explicit set of standards and values, Bridges' (1989) concerns are important in highlighting the difficulties inherent in incorporating assessments of qualities with those of achievements and abilities.

Furthermore, concentration on personal qualities, in the form of character traits seems to miss the whole point about holistic assessment (Fairbairn 1988), in that such traits need to be seen in a wider context. For example, descriptors 9.5, 9.6 and 9.7 may refer to individual social qualities; but on the other hand they may be evidence of problems at home or at school which could require attention. However, it is fair to say that many Benton staff saw the inclusion of descriptors relating to personal and social qualities, not as an opportunity to judge pupils, but as a chance to talk through and discuss things which were of importance to their development or their lives in general.

As such, the actual dialogue was regarded as the most important thing and was seen to have beneficial results. The extent to which this was the case with all Benton pupils, however, is debatable; but many staff seemed to assume that there were properties intrinsic to the negotiation process which meant that it was equally beneficial to all pupils. In cases discussed earlier, however, it has been shown how extended negotiation sessions were experienced by high ability extrovert pupils (Charlotte and Louise), whilst some staff had difficulty in remembering the names of 'quiet little girls'. The possibility that the negotiation sessions with their emphasis on oral and more general social skills, could favour extrovert pupils with lots to talk about and work against more introverted, shy pupils was not explicitly considered by staff at Benton School. Given that Records of Achievement are produced by a process which recognizes and seeks to account for individual pupil differences, it would seem contradictory to expect all pupils to have similar positive experiences of them. As will be shown later, for some pupils the prospect of engaging in a one-to-one discussion with a member of staff was in itself threatening and militated against open discussion between the two parties.

The negotiation room

A physical manifestation of negotiation existed in Benton School by means of a small room which had been set aside and furnished solely for that purpose. Negotiation periods appeared on staff timetables and corresponding lists of times for use of the negotiation room were given prominent position on the main staff notice-board. Not only did this serve to ensure that staff kept to their allotted times in the room but it also helped to maintain a high profile for Records of Achievement in the school generally. References to the negotiation room were common and all pupils seemed to know where it was, were familiar with it, and knew what went on within it.

The deputy head explained that the reason for the conversion of a spare room into the negotiation room was to provide an area which was secure and conducive to genuine dialogue between teacher and pupil. In his view the negotiation room provided the right environment for discussion between the two parties on the basis, as far as possible, of equality. The 'official' rationale for the room was that it represented a form of neutral ground away from the classroom where pupils could feel free to express opinions and discuss issues openly and confidently, without fear of recrimination or of being exposed to other members of staff or their class-mates. For example, if a pupil felt that the reason for his or her poor performance in a particular subject was due to a failure to get on with a teacher, or put at its most basic, to poor teaching, then he or she would be encouraged to discuss this in a sensible and constructive manner in the confines of the negotiation room. The deputy head described the negotiation room enthusiastically thus:

> So we've got this thing called the negotiation room, and the majority of negotiations go on there. You know we've got easy chairs in there and there's a potted plant in there, and there's a table, and the computer and hopefully it's conducive to the negotiation environment.

In spite of the easy chairs and potted plant, however, the extent to which an atmosphere of equality and balance between teacher and pupil may be achieved remained questionable. For example, interviews with pupils revealed very few who felt in any sense on a par with members of staff. Several pupils admitted to finding the room threatening, merely by the fact that they were in such close proximity with their teacher. One pupil insisted on keeping the door of the room open during negotiation sessions, because of a feeling of claustrophobia. On another occasion a fifth-year pupil referred to the room as 'Cell Block H', a reference to an Australian television soap opera about a prison!

Clearly, enthusiasm for the room was not shared by all. If pupils felt uncomfortable in the room, which after all was a strange environment to them within the school, then the extent to which they were able to discuss with teachers as an equal partner must be called into question. Furthermore, the suggestion by one pupil that the room could be compared to a prison cell raises the question of control in negotiation sessions. If the physical environment is felt to contribute to such a feeling by the pupils then questions about the extent to which the negotiation room is conducive to an atmosphere of equality between teacher and pupil must surely be posed. Similarly, it may also be appropriate to consider the extent to which the room and the negotiation sessions *per se* contributed to greater discipline in the school (cf. Hitchcock 1986). For example, was the negotiation room seen by pupils as the place where they go to be told what to do, as one member of staff put it 'to be put on the right track'? In this situation, notions of a treatment room (cf. Orwell 1949) are evoked, to which pupils are taken in order that they may discuss their shortcomings and difficulties. For some pupils this clearly was the case. Where performance in lessons had been poor over the intervening period since their last negotiation session, there may have been little to celebrate in terms of achievement. Similarly, where there had been difficulties with a pupil in terms of discipline the negotiation session offered an opportunity for staff to discuss these difficulties and so encourage better behaviour. In either of these situations the notion of some sort of parity of status between teacher and pupil was surely illusory. In the negotiation room the pupil had no option but to sit and listen to the teacher.

Managing the negotiation

In all negotiation sessions it was the teacher who managed and directed the conversation, usually in accordance with the computer package holding the descriptors. The teacher also decided when the negotiation session would take place, at what time of the school year, and usually it was the teacher who decided when the session should end and thereby decided how long it should last. Clearly, it was the teacher who controlled the negotiations. Throughout the school, there was, nevertheless, a rhetoric which saw the negotiation session as the only time when teachers and pupils could talk to each other as equals in the teaching and learning partnership. At the same time, however, the terminology which surrounded and defined the negotiation sessions referred to the teacher as 'the negotiator'. Similarly, pupils were referred to as having been 'negotiated'. The everyday and unquestioning use of these terms served to reinforce the position of the pupil as the object of the negotiation sessions rather than an equal partner in the process. Negotiation was something which was done to the pupils rather than something in which they were equal partners.

Nevertheless, many of the Benton staff, and the head in particular, saw one of the great strengths of the Record of Achievement process and especially the negotiation sessions in terms of its capacity to improve relations between teachers and pupils. The head, David Fox, asserted that negotiation sessions were important in developing an atmosphere of trust and rapport between teacher and pupil. He stated:

> In the main, with the vast majority of children and certainly the great majority of teachers, relationships between teacher and pupil in this school have improved considerably since we started negotiating Records of Achievement. I mean a lot of the children say a lot of very confidential things in the negotiations, and you create an air of trust and confidentiality with a member of staff which you never created between pupil and teacher before.

From this position of trust, David Fox believed that enormous contributions could be made to the teaching and learning process and to the motivation of pupils, encouraging them to take responsibility for their own learning, and to feel that they were an important part of the school. My field notes from the first meeting with David Fox recorded his enthusiasm for Records of Achievement, and demonstrated his belief that they may contribute to the good of the school in a whole range of ways. My notes were as follows:

> The head explains that Records of Achievement have now become an integral part of the school. He describes the benefits as 'enormous'. He sees them as a panacea for many things which were wrong with the school and enthusiastically lists their contribution to:

- better teacher–pupil relations;
- improved pupil behaviour;
- greater integration of pupils with school aims and objectives;
- less litter and graffiti about the school;
- enhanced pupil motivation;
- more appropriate assessment and learning strategies;
- pupils taking responsibility for their own learning.

The key to all of these improvements was seen as negotiation, as rapport and trust between teacher and pupil.

Whilst David Fox did not wish to imply that teacher–pupil relations were particularly poor prior to the introduction of Records of Achievement, or that dialogue between the parties did not take place, he believed they provided a structure for them. By the identification of a process, a degree of uniformity and systematization was added to teacher–pupil relations which no longer meant that their success depended entirely on the personalities of those involved. As every pupil was scheduled for a negotiation session, this meant they had the opportunity for individual discussion which would enable them to be viewed independently of any group to which they belonged.

The emphasis on the individual would seem to be where the strength of the negotiation session rested and in this sense it was perhaps less important that there should be a situation of equality between teacher and pupil and more important that there was an opportunity for pupils to receive individual attention from teachers and not least an occasion when difficulties as well as success could be discussed. In most schools the opportunity for pupils to receive uninterrupted attention from staff is rare. Teaching and learning in an English school is an essentially collective activity. As such, the half an hour negotiation session for the Record of Achievement has the potential to make a valuable contribution to the individual development of the pupil.

Many claims about the positive contribution of the negotiation sessions were made by the head and staff; it should not be assumed, however, that their introduction and development had been without difficulty. For example, the question of time for effective negotiation and the pressure this placed on staff has already been discussed. Time represented perhaps the most easily identified difficulty associated with the development of a whole school approach to Records of Achievement, but in the course of this research a range of issues emerged which brought to light difficulties and challenges associated with their development. Moreover, some of the issues which staff and pupils identified showed how negotiation in particular had become an important theme throughout the school and in this sense, was about more than just the 30-minute discussion session held annually between teacher and pupil. Before discussing the wider assimilation of negotiation into the school culture, however, it will be useful to consider the actual experience of the formal negotiation session from the perspective of the pupils and teachers.

Experiencing negotiation

During the time that I spent in Benton School numerous conversations amongst staff were overheard or participated in, during which statements about negotiation were common. Similarly, during interviews with pupils the term negotiation was in constant use, as they spoke in terms of 'being negotiated'. By implication, the frequent use of the term implied a common understanding of its definition. As was shown earlier, however, the one-to-one discussion sessions were often characterized by agreement between teacher and pupil rather than disagreement. In such situations the extent to which any negotiation was required was limited. More than one pupil recalled a situation where their one-to-one sessions had been characterized by staff and student identifying the same descriptors which were thought to best describe the student's progress and performance over the academic year. There then resulted a period of discussion between the two parties about a wide range of issues relating to both school and non-school activities.

In such situations it would seem more appropriate to refer to the sessions as discussion, rather than negotiation sessions. Where agreement was common the need for compromise either by teacher or pupil, or both, was reduced. The term 'negotiation' with its industrial and international bargaining connotations implied a situation of confrontation between the two parties, in this case between teacher and pupil (Evans 1989). In order to reach some kind of acceptable compromise one or both sides must give way until a situation of bargained corporatism (Crouch 1979) could be achieved. The term 'negotiation' implied, therefore, a situation in which disagreement occurred which in order to be resolved required some form of exchange between the parties. Hargreaves *et al.* (1988) take issue with those commentators who suggest that negotiation is a term more akin to industrial relations than education. Adopting the definition of 'open negotiation' developed by Woods (1983: 133):

> . . . where parties are aware of the contract, move some way to meet each other of their own volition and subsequently arrive at a consensus.

Hargreaves *et al.* suggest that this definition enables the differences in power and experience which exist between teacher and pupil and which pervade the exercise, to be kept in mind. In this respect he sees terms like 'dialogue' and 'discussion' which have found favour with the DES, as 'emotionally soothing and descriptively inaccurate'.

Whilst Hargreaves is clear in his assessment of power relations, he fails to engage with the possibility of agreement between teacher and pupil. As we have seen, Benton pupils often recalled instances of agreement with their teachers and perhaps because of the use of the term 'negotiation', these instances often resulted in no discussion or dialogue. Surely, the use of the term discussion or dialogue would allow for verbal exchange between teacher and pupil regardless of whether there was agreement or not and also accommodate differences in status and power. Furthermore, Hargreaves *et al.* (1988) assert that the term 'negotiation' is a constant reminder of the inequalities of power and experience which pervade the Record of Achievement process and a reminder that such inequalities need to be confronted and dealt with positively. Whilst one can accept this need, the continued use of the term 'negotiation' with its implicit agenda of confrontation tempered by structural inequalities, must surely contribute to a perpetuation of the situation which Hargreaves wishes to challenge. By emphasizing the term 'negotiation' in the context of inequality, pupils must be aware that they will usually be the ones who have to do the negotiating.

In some teacher–pupil discussion sessions there were difficulties where pupil and teacher held different views of the latter's achievement and progress. In such situations it may have been necessary for teacher and pupil to negotiate over the selection of the appropriate descriptor, from the hierarchically arranged descriptor list (see Appendix 1), which was seen to be most appropriate in describing the pupil's achievement and progress. It was only in situations like this that the term 'negotiation' was appropriate. Its common use to describe all teacher–pupil discussions must be seen as a misuse of the term. Clearly in many pupil–teacher discussion sessions there was a high degree of consensus over the choice of descriptors and negotiation did not arise. Alternatively, evidence from pupils suggested that some staff ruled out any possibility of negotiation; and, as will be shown later, they insisted that pupils accept their choice of descriptor regardless of the pupil's own view of the situation. Where this occurred it would again be inappropriate to refer to the situation as a negotiation session.

James (1989a) also engages with the question of negotiation or dialogue. She asserts that the debate is not merely one of semantics but relates to the different activities of formative and summative assessment which are intrinsic to the Record of Achievement process. She states:

> In other words, formative dialogue could be expected to contribute to understanding and development, while summatively oriented negotiation should aim to promote credibility, accountability and justice.
>
> (p. 151)

Although in raising this dichotomy James is seeking to 'end some of the muddle that threatens the baby as well as the bath-water', it would seem that she is actually doing the opposite. The use of two terms must surely serve to complicate the negotiation/dialogue debate further.

Overall, the evidence from Benton School suggests that the one-to-one negotiation sessions might be better termed 'discussion sessions'. This would avoid the misuse of the term 'negotiation' and at the same time encourage dialogue between teacher and pupil, whether or not there is agreement.

Status and position

In the opinion of David Fox, the Benton headteacher, Records of Achievement had been responsible for wide-scale changes in the school. In his view, schooling had ceased to be something which was done to pupils and was now an activity in which teachers and pupils participated together. Pupils of Benton were no longer passive recipients of information, they were active and more equal partners in the education process. As evidence of this the head pointed not only to greater respect shown by pupils to school buildings and properties but also to enhanced communication skills and a willingness on the part of the pupils to converse with adults on equal terms. This greater maturity, the head believed, existed not only in the pupils' relationships with adults outside school but also in their relationship with Benton staff. Indeed, the very philosophy upon which the Benton Record of Achievement was based stressed a need for greater equilibrium and reciprocity between teachers and pupils. For example, in terms of the negotiation sessions teachers and pupils were in theory equal partners. The teacher could not impose his or her decisions on the pupil and the pupil's opinions and arguments were to be attributed similar status to those of the staff.

Reaching a situation where pupils and teachers saw themselves as more or less equal partners was not without difficulties. The traditional role of the teacher as disciplinarian and as the purveyor of knowledge to pupils, located power and control in the teacher–pupil relationship firmly with the teacher. In seeking to bring about a situation of greater balance between the two parties the Record of Achievement could be seen to be attempting to bring about fundamental changes. Indeed, if Records of Achievement were to bring about such changes to teaching and learning and to the way in which pupils viewed their contribution to this process, then they required wide-scale changes in staff–student relationships and in the approach to reporting and recording in the first place. For example, Records of Achievement encourage pupils to be assertive, to engage in dialogue with teachers and when appropriate, to ask questions about the role of the teacher and the processes of teaching and learning. In order for pupils to adopt such behaviour and for it to be accepted and used positively by teachers, the teacher must no longer be viewed as a distant unapproachable figure but as an equal partner in the education process. As part of this teachers would be encouraged to look critically upon their own role. David Fox explained that not all Benton teachers had found these required changes easy to cope with. He stated:

> You see all of this business of negotiating with children in Records of Achievement and changing your classroom practice, to get out from behind your desk and amongst children, and putting yourself in, as they [the teachers] see it, a less secure position; it's very worrying to some traditional teachers.

Clearly, the head believed there had been fundamental changes in teacher–pupil relations as a result of Records of Achievement, in particular the teacher–pupil negotiation sessions. Moreover, it would seem that he regarded the provision of the physical environment by means of the negotiation room, and the ethos which had developed around the negotiation sessions as central to affecting fundamental changes to the way in which teachers and pupils looked upon each other and to the way in which they approached teaching and learning. However, data collected from interviews with pupils throughout this research revealed some considerable distance between what may be seen as the rhetoric of teacher–pupil partnership and the reality of teacher directed negotiation sessions or put more crudely, between the perceptions of the head and some teachers and the experiences of the pupils. For example, the pupils revealed that during the negotiation sessions the form teacher was invariably the one who took the lead by doing most of the talking and deciding how much time could be spent discussing a particular point. Furthermore, the use of the specific battery of descriptors which drove the discussion actually defined the content of the negotiations to a large degree. Moreover, the pupils' experiences revealed quite clearly that not only was agreement deemed to reduce the need for discussion but it also meant that the teacher could drive the session quickly through the descriptors. My conversation with Simon, a fifth-year pupil, was enlightening in this respect:

> CP: When you are in the negotiation room who does most of the talking, you or the teacher?
>
> *Simon*: Well if you agree on everything it's the teacher because he's just going through [the descriptor sheets] saying 'yeah, right, that's agreed' and he just keeps going until you don't agree.

Clearly, in this situation the teacher is in control. The process is driven by agreement and the emphasis is placed on the pupil to stop it or slow it down by disagreement. In this situation it would be possible for a pupil who constantly stopped the process to be characterized as obstructive or difficult. Where teachers had a large number of negotiations to get through, constant 'interruptions' may have proved difficult to cope with in the allotted time. As a consequence, and certainly in the case of Simon, it would appear that the pupil only participated where he or she was able to take the initiative by stopping the teacher. In this context, the pupil was required to wrest control from the teacher. Whilst Simon was sufficiently confident and articulate to do this, not all pupils were. Furthermore, as two more fifth-year pupils, Paul and Sally, described, attempts to do this were not always successful. Their experiences of negotiation with their form tutor revealed a situation which was in no way characterized by any sense of equality or reciprocity. They recalled:

CP: Have either of you been in a situation where you couldn't agree?
Sally: Yes, I have.
CP: What happens then?
Sally: Well, Mr Shaw just batters you down.
CP: Batters you down?
Sally: Yes, say you've got like six against one [i.e. the opinion of six teachers to one pupil]. Like I put two [descriptor No. 2] and they put four, Mr Shaw just talks you round.

Although the actual negotiation sessions take place on a one-to-one basis, the teacher comes to the session equipped with information, collected from colleagues about the pupil's performance and achievement in every subject. As Paul and Sally relate, the information held by the teacher is used as evidence, against which they have to argue. Our conversation continued:

CP: Is it difficult to argue with six against one?
Paul: Yes it is a bit.
Sally: It's annoying because they are all teachers and if they don't agree you can't say a lot about it because . . .
Paul: Because there are six of them and just you.
Sally: Yes, [about] school work you can't really talk them down because they are teachers.

For Paul and Sally it is the status of teacher which is important and the number of the teachers against which they have to argue.

Sally's comment '. . . you can't really talk them down because they are teachers' conveys the concepts of status and hierarchy which have been interpreted as barriers or limits to negotiation. Moreover, the capacity of the form tutor to call upon information provided by all the teachers with whom the pupils have contact, served to reinforce the teacher's power and control of the negotiation session. As Paul explained, this made any suggestion of equality between teacher and pupil or parity of opinion illusory. Our conversation continued thus:

CP: I thought when you came in here [the negotiation room] you were supposed to be on the same level, more or less equal.

Paul: You are, but it's psychological really: When you've got six teachers against you, you think they must be right. It would be best if he didn't say how many teachers were against you. If he just said that some people said that, or the majority said.

In the face of such opposition, despite being an academically bright and articulate pupil, Paul felt unable to influence the situation. In the words of Sally, he was just 'battered down'.

The experiences of Paul and Sally reinforce notions of control and confrontation in the negotiation sessions. If teachers are seen to 'batter' pupils down and to present staff views in a quantitative way against which pupils have to argue, how far can the negotiation session be seen as one of equilibrium, where the view of teachers and pupils are attributed similar status?

Bridges (1989) discusses the problem of status inequality in one-to-one negotiations. He puts forward a number of ways in which 'pupils' hands could be strengthed' in negotiation sessions. He suggests:

- Pupils could be given personal support in the form of, for example, a sympathetic friend or another teacher in the role of advocate committed to supporting the pupil's position in the negotiation.
- Structures could be devised which armed pupils with rewards or sanctions, e.g. pupil assessment by the teacher could be linked with teacher assessment by the pupil.
- Pupils could be given training designed to enable them

courteously but firmly to stand their ground in negotiations – not unlike, perhaps, some of the training offered as part of a health education programme in how to say 'no' to friends persuading you to have a sniff or a cigarette.

(p. 126)

Whilst such strategies may enjoy a degree of success they would also require fundamental changes to the purpose and nature of negotation sessions. For example, linking Records of Achievement to staff appraisal by pupils would surely shift the focus from pupil achievements to teacher performance. An interesting strategy, but difficult to assimilate to the aims and purpose of Records of Achievement.

Having located power in negotiation firmly with the teachers, it should not be assumed that all negotiation sessions operated in the same way, or that the teacher always had the upper hand in deciding which descriptor was agreed upon in every negotiation session. For example, David, a fifth-year pupil, recalled a situation which involved negotiation and compromise both on his behalf and that of the teacher before a statement which was acceptable to both of them was reached. Our conversation brought to light an interesting process.

CP: Right, so if you come to the negotiation session with some ideas about yourself and the teacher has other ideas, what happens then?

David: Well you discuss it for a while and finally you come to some agreement.

CP: Have you ever had a disagreement with a teacher over a descriptor?

David: Yes, I did once, but we eventually resolved it. I think it was about library skills, I thought I was pretty good at that.

CP: Library skills?

David: Yeah, it was finding books in the library, using their codes and that, and the teachers commented, and they put me lower down than I thought I was. And so eventually we middled it out.

CP: Middled it out?

David: Well sort of, I went down and he came up, we compromised.

In this situation the disagreement seems to have been resolved without great difficulty. Furthermore, David's use of the term 'middled out' is interesting, and may be seen as a direct reference to the physical appearance of the descriptor sheets which form the basis for negotiation.

Descriptors are grouped together in relation to the specific skill or quality to which they are addressed, and are arranged hierarchically in descending order. For example, the descriptors for reading ability are presented to the pupil thus:

6.0 Reading
6.1 Reads and understands material presented in a variety of written forms.
6.2 Follows successfully a series of written instructions and uses when necessary everyday reference sources, e.g. dictionary.
6.3 Reads and understands basic instructions, notices and messages.
6.4 Reads and understands simple written material with assistance.
6.5 Is unable to use alphabetical lists or to organize written material properly.
6.6 Finds difficulty in understanding any kind of written material even with assistance.

In terms of David's compromise, therefore, middling out would involve him dropping from 6.2 to 6.3, and the teacher raising his opinion from 6.4 to 6.3. In David's case the organization of the descriptors in the hierarchical form clearly influenced the process of negotiation and compromise. The descriptor lists provided the teacher and pupil with ready-made statements which could be identified and discussed before teacher and pupil agreed to their inclusion in the Record of Achievement.

Although David's example of compromise is one in which it was necessary for the pupil to accept a 'lower' view of himself and hence agree to the use of a 'lower' descriptor, such cases were not particularly common. Several members of staff stressed that the reverse of this situation occurred more frequently. In short, pupils would hold their achievements and abilities in lower esteem than their teachers did. When this occurred teachers usually encouraged pupils to identify and accept a higher descriptor. For example, Jane Upton, a third-year tutor, recalled many circumstances where this was the case. She stated:

JU: I find that in 90 per cent of the cases they [the pupils]
         actually underestimate what they are capable of doing.
CP: So what happens then?
JU: You have to convince them really.

Persuading pupils to accept higher descriptors was seen not merely
as a mean of recognizing their achievement, but also as a way
of encouraging pupils. The choice and discussion of a particular
descriptor may have been as much about motivating the pupil to
achieve further success as about celebrating what had already been
achieved. Alternatively, staff also spoke in terms of identifying
a lower descriptor than the pupil might have thought appropriate
in order to avoid complacency. In this respect, the descriptors
provided the teachers with a strategy for enhancing as well as
recognizing pupil achievement. Again this reinforced the notion of
Records of Achievement as tools for manipulation by teachers.
Whilst this may be to the benefit of the pupils, it again calls in to
question issues of equality.

The case of John, a fifth year, showed that convincing pupils
to accept higher descriptors was not necessarily straightforward.
In explaining why he refused to sign his Record of Achievement
at the end of a negotiation session he remarked:

John: Well, it was about exams sort of thing. I put I don't
            do my best work in exams and they [the teachers] put
            I do my best work. And in the end you know, it went
            on for ages I tried to talk him [the teacher conducting
            the negotiation session] round, and he tried to talk me
            round his way and we agreed in the end.
CP: So why wouldn't you agree with him?
John: Well, I was just saying I thought I could have done
            better in my exams.

In John's case there was a reluctance to accept the teacher's view,
and considerable persuasion was required by the teacher before
agreement could be reached (cf. Woods 1983). The example is
illustrative of the complexity with which the identification of
descriptors might be imbued. Whilst John's form tutor saw the
descriptors as a means of recognizing achievement in examinations
John was concerned that the descriptors would reflect not only
what had been achieved, but also what could be achieved. From

John's point of view they were not merely summative statements, but statements about his potential to achieve in examinations.

In this respect the negotiation session was not perceived by the pupil as an opportunity to score points from the teachers by negotiating 'inflated' Records of Achievement. All the evidence from Benton teachers and pupils suggests that this was rarely the case and that, overall, pupils had a fairly good idea of their own achievements and abilities which they brought to the negotiation sessions. Alan Neville, a teacher with several years' experience of the Benton Record of Achievement summed up the situation in the following terms:

> . . . the children assess themselves almost 100 per cent. They assess themselves the way teachers do. They don't sort of try to pull the wool over your eyes, I mean you get the odd one in a hundred might that's all.

Whilst it is likely that most members of staff would agree with Alan Neville's comment, Mavis Johnson, a fourth-year tutor, did recall some limited difficulty with pupils over inflated egos. She explained:

> . . . the only difficulties I've ever had, and this may sound very sexist, is with arrogant males who think they're wonderful and the staff don't. The girls tend to underestimate themselves and put themselves lower if anything or are very honest and see themselves in the right way. The boys on the whole are fine except for these few who have got this ego thing who think they are marvellous.

Where there are difficulties with pupils attempting to 'score points' over their teachers Mavis Johnson's experience suggests this may be gender related. If this suggestion is linked with comments quoted earlier from Susan Watts, a part-time teacher, about difficulties of getting to know 'quiet little girls', then it may be appropriate to pose questions about the extent to which the negotiation process is male orientated. Whilst there is no evidence to suggest that male pupils necessarily have a more positive Record of Achievement experience, some staff comments have indicated that where girls are not assertive the process may to some extent, neglect them. Similarly, work by Torrance (1988) highlights a tendency for girls to underestimate their achievements in situations of self-assessment, whilst boys identify a need to get the highest mark possible. Torrance's interviewees made the following remarks:

> *Girl*: . . . you always used to undermark yourself in case the teacher thought it wasn't good enough . . .
>
> *Boy*: I think you should put the highest mark you can, you know, let's face it, this is to do with your future . . .
>
> (Torrance 1988: 5)

Unless tutors are aware of what may be a tendency towards female modesty, some of the girls' achievements may go unrecognized and their personal development undervalued.

Ultimately, if pupils and teachers were unable to reach agreement over the identification of descriptors, pupils could refuse to sign their Record of Achievement documentation which demonstrated that statements had been agreed by a process of teacher–pupil dialogue. In Benton School this rarely happened. Where it did, the year head or headteacher would be involved in an attempt to reach a compromise. This was seen to be particularly important in relation to the final fifth-year negotiation session. Agreed statements between teachers and pupils formed an important part of the summative Document of Record. Pupils were encouraged to use this document when seeking employment or entry to higher education (see Chapter 6). Most pupils would be reluctant, therefore, to leave school without some kind of agreed statement signed by themselves and a teacher, even if serious disagreements had been encountered during negotiation sessions. In relation to this Mavis Johnson recalled a situation where considerable compromise had to take place before an agreed statement could be produced. She explained:

> . . . I had terrible problems with two boys because at the time we had on it . . . calm, polite, there was a whole list of things like these qualities . . . and these boys maintained they were polite and the staff could not agree and so in the end, this shows how silly they were, they agreed to have printed on the bottom of their actual document of record, this is the final thing, 'Ian feels that he is polite but the staff cannot agree with him'. They agreed to have that on rather than nothing.

Although Mavis Johnson saw the boys' decision as silly, the opinion of the pupil was upheld and an agreed statement was produced.

The addition of the staff view, however, may have seriously undermined that opinion and in that sense may have been construed as a negative statement. Nevertheless, negotiation did take place and a conclusion resulted.

Descriptor language

The research has also highlighted concern over the language in which the descriptors were expressed. Concern was apparent on two levels. In the first instances several pupils explained that they simply could not understand the words and phrases with which the descriptors were constructed. Phillip, a fourth-year pupil explained:

> Sometimes you don't understand them [descriptors] because they are quite difficult to understand, you can put down the wrong things.

Not understanding the descriptors meant that pupils sometimes had difficulty in differentiating between statements. Again Phillip explained:

> Some of them are very close, what they mean, but then Mr Reid [his form tutor] knows that they've got a slightly different meaning. So you have to ask sometimes.

Not all pupils were prepared to ask staff to differentiate between descriptors for fear of being judged to be unintelligent as Maria, a fifth year, recalled during our conversation.

> CP: So what happens if you don't understand one of the phrases?
> Maria: You just tick it, just tick whatever. You could leave it out if you wanted to, but if you thought you understood you'd tick it. And Mr Jones would say, 'Do you really think this is you?' You often find it undermines you. I think the questions are a bit too complicated.

In this case, the descriptors which had been designed to aid communication, acted to undermine the pupil or to cause her to pass over issues which were not understood without due consideration or discussion.

Allied to this difficulty was the problem of descriptors being so similar in their wording as to make differentiation between them very difficult. For example, under the heading 'work and study skills' pupils were required to select one descriptor under the subheading 'Oral Explanation'. The list was as follows:

4.0 Oral explanation
4.1 Presents a lengthy, fluent, reasoned argument.
4.2 Clearly explains a complex process.
4.3 Explains a process clearly and accurately.
4.4 Explains what he/she is doing.
4.5 Has a very limited vocabulary and finds it difficult to explain clearly what he/she is doing.
4.6 Is very reluctant to attempt oral explanation except in very informal situations.

Hargreaves *et al.* (1988) assert that one of the best ways of testing a Record of Achievement is to complete it for oneself. Taking his advice, I find it difficult to opt for any one statement from 4.1 to 4.4 in isolation. For example, if one were to opt for 4.2 then one would imply an inability to present a lengthy, fluent and reasoned argument. Similarly, 4.2 implies that the ability to 'clearly explain a complex process' demands a higher level of skill than that which is required for 4.3 'Explains a process, clearly and accurately'. To differentiate between these descriptors is difficult. Moreover, the list is confusing in so far as it brings together different kinds of skills and abilities and asks the pupil to choose between them. For example, the skills required to present a fluent argument are very different from those required to explain a complex process. Argument and explanation are not the same kinds of constructs and it seems, therefore, erroneous to place them in the same hierarchy. The list implies that reasoned argument requires a higher level of ability than complex explanation. It may be asserted that to provide a clear explanation of a complex process, a high level of understanding of the process is first of all required. The ability to grasp and then convey that understanding may in many circumstances, outweigh that required to present a reasoned argument of say, a fairly straightforward issue.

   The problem in this particular case is two-fold and illustrative of the difficulties inherent in descriptor banks. In the first instance it is assumed that those who complete and use the descriptor sheets will share the same understanding of them as those who are responsible for their construction. Secondly, they assume that skills, abilities and qualities can be placed neatly in hierarchies to be isolated and identified without serious problems of overlap. In doing this, the descriptor list ascribes greater status to some skills than to others. The basis upon which it does this, however, is not made clear.

Returning to the suggestion of Hargreaves *et al.* (1988) that one should try to complete the bank of descriptors oneself, I found myself repeatedly qualifying my selections with the words 'it depends' or 'sometimes'. For example, again under the heading 'work and study skills' the following list is offered from which pupils are required to choose one descriptor:

1.0 Working with others
1.1 Recognizes the needs of the group and is prepared to take a positive lead.
1.2 Well motivated in group activities.
1.3 Is prepared to work with others when given a task.
1.4 Prefers to work on his/her own whenever possible.
1.5 Finds it difficult to work with other people.
1.6 Can be disruptive in a working-group situation.
1.7 Is compelled to work alone so that the group can progress unhindered.

Whilst my ego directs me towards selecting 1.1, I must also consider carefully 1.5. Surely, there are times when everyone finds it difficult to work with other people. Quite simply, it depends what the task is and who the other people are. The hierarchy implies, however, that descriptor 1.5 shows more failings in my personal work and study skills than does descriptor 1.1. By this criteria many PhD mathematics students, for example, who often prefer to work on their own whenever possible (descriptor 1.4) would be seemed to have substandard work and study skills. Clearly, the response to this issue depends on the task, the situation and the people. It again highlights the difficulties of assessing particular skills and abilities without a specific context.

Presented in these hierarchical terms, the prescriptive descriptor bank seems unable to accommodate the variations necessary to provide an accurate picture of the ability, qualities and skills of all individuals. To assume that six or seven statements can provide sufficient range for all abilities and cope with overlap and ambiguity of definition is to misunderstand the complexities of human achievement. In their defence, those responsible for devising and using descriptor bank systems claim that individual statements were not intended to stand alone, but were to facilitate discussion of the very ambiguities which they embody. The experiences of Benton teachers and pupils suggest, however, that discussion does not always occur over every descriptor. Where there is agreement between teacher and pupil, or where there is pressure to complete negotiation sessions as quickly as possible, then discussion may be at a minimum. Agreement does not, however, guarantee understanding and scarcity of time may mean pupils are denied the opportunity to make sure that they have selected the correct descriptor.

Descriptor numbers

Descriptors in the Benton Record of Achievement were arranged hierarchically. Each descriptor was then attributed with a number. For example:

2.0 Ability to work independently
2.1 Shows outstanding capacity for organizing his/her work and time effectively.
2.2 Shows a considerable capacity for organizing his/her work and time effectively.
. . .
2.8 Does not show much inclination to spend time in organizing his/her work effectively.

This had implications for the extent to which negotiation took place over qualitative statements as opposed to numerical labels. Staff and pupils were discouraged by the head and senior staff from referring to descriptors solely in relation to their place on the list (e.g. 2.1, 2.2, 2.8). In the opinion of one teacher the very existence of the numbering system meant that the quality of teacher–pupil discussion was adversely affected. He explained:

> We have this interesting numbering system so we stop talking about the actual criteria and start talking about numbers, and then they lose their value.

It is interesting that what was presented as an aid to negotiation, may have acted to reduce the amount of discussion which occurred.

Although this fear was not expressed by more than one member of staff, the extent to which staff and pupils referred to descriptors purely by numbers reinforced the point he made.

For example the following excerpt from an interview with a games teacher is one illustration of a style of conversation that had become fairly commonplace in Benton School.

> . . . suppose they [the teachers] had all gone for 3. Suppose he [the pupil] had 2.2, 2.3, 2.4 and they compromised at 2.7. Well I'd say his opinion of himself doesn't match what, you know, most of the teaching staff see him as.

This teacher clearly felt at ease referring to particular descriptors by their numbers, and had a good understanding of their position in the Record of Achievement hierarchy. Whether the pupils shared this understanding, or like me were a little confused, is a point for consideration. Whilst it is possible to follow the logic of the statement there is no means of understanding its meaning without reference to a list of descriptors. The numbers provided a shorthand at the expense of meaning. This example demonstrates the importance of language to effective discussion. By referring merely to numbers there could be no assurance that teachers and pupils had a shared understanding of the individual descriptors.

Informal negotiation

So far discussion of negotiation has been limited to the 'official', planned negotiation which was required by the Record of Achievement process. However, conversations with staff and pupils during my time in Benton School revealed that the language and the concept of negotiation had entered many areas of school life. For example, members of staff were frequently overheard using the term 'negotiate' in their everyday conversations with colleagues. For example, a teacher responsible for organizing a games team told a colleague from another school that he had phoned him to 'negotiate' the use of some fourth-year pupils in a third-year match. Similarly, the deputy head explained how he had to 'negotiate' access to the negotiation room in order to use it for that very purpose. He recalled:

> I've seen people who've been trudging round trying to find
> a place to do negotiation and we've had this old computer
> room upstairs for a long time but they wanted to put the
> nimbus network in there . . . So what we did was I negotiated
> with the member of staff concerned and we've now moved the
> [Nimbus] right along . . . and now that's the negotiating room.

The point to be drawn from these two examples is that the term
negotiation has become part of the everyday vocabulary of the
school, and the concept embedded even in mundane activities.
However, the extent to which negotiation actually took place in
either of these situations may also be open to question. For example,
there was little bargaining between the sides and no discussion or
consideration of any sanctions which one side may mount against
the other in an attempt to secure the desired outcome. In this sense,
it would seem that the term negotiation was again used to describe
discussion between two parties and to refer to administrative
arrangements.

Further evidence of the extent to which negotiation had
permeated the school could be seen from a field note made after
a conversation held with Shirley Price, a year head.

> One problem of negotiation in Records of Achievement as
> perceived by Shirley Price is its overspill into other areas of
> the school and into education in general. This has meant that
> some fundamental school rules have been questioned. For
> example, she stated that some pupils felt they should be able
> to negotiate on school uniform and behaviour. She felt this
> was probably inevitable given the emphasis which was placed
> on negotiation in the school, and the skills that this
> encouraged in the pupils.

Whilst Shirley Price was a keen supporter of Records of
Achievement she had concerns about the effects of negotiation
on the position of the teacher and on the school in general. These
concerns were shared by Jane Upton, a third-year tutor, and again
a supporter of Records of Achievement. She explained:

> *JU:* Some kids, the problem kids, as in behaviour problem
> wise, try to take advantage of this [the emphasis on
> negotiation] and because they have got the laws to
> negotiate, they negotiate in other areas of the school.

CP: How do you mean?

JU: Well, you get a situation whereby it's a straight down the road situation and you will discipline them. They would then stand there and try to negotiate with you. And you say 'Look you've done something wrong, you have to take the punishment for that, there is no negotiation here. You've done something that you were not allowed to do' and they will stand there giving it, you know, which I don't find we had before. I mean I might be wrong but I sense that's all come up since we started all this.

For Jane Upton this was seen as a negative and unacceptable use of negotiation. However, in terms of encouraging pupils to communicate with teachers as equals, to take responsibility for their own actions and generally to stand up for themselves, such behaviour could be seen as a successful and desirable consequence of Records of Achievement. What Jane Upton's comments show is that clear limits exist to negotiation and the situations in which it may be attempted. Furthermore, it would seem that the decision of when and in what situations negotiation can be practised rests with the teachers.

Instances where pupils attempted to 'break the rules' of negotiation were not common and Jane Upton went on to outline her belief that Records of Achievement were a means by which general school discipline could be improved. She explained:

I see a difference in them. I see them getting more open and willing to talk about things. They are more willing to talk about their problems which has got to be an advantage, because that way you can build up something and if you know them they are a lot easier to discipline and control. And you can't teach them if they're not controlled.

What is interesting here is that Jane Upton sees Records of Achievement as a means of encouraging pupils to become more assertive by becoming more open and willing to talk, yet at the same time they are also a means by which teachers can exert greater control over their pupils. Like many Benton staff, Jane Upton saw positive effects of the overspill of the Record of Achievement process into other areas of schooling. For example, pupils were seen to be more willing to take responsibility for their own behaviour and the consequences of it; and in particular the head saw the 'overspill' of negotiation as an illustration that pupils were actually thinking about their behaviour. He stated:

> I think it's a healthy thing if a kid comes up and says 'Why do we wear a uniform?' And then you try and explain historically why we wear school uniform . . . I think that if the pupils are viewing some things as being negotiated then in a way that's not a bad thing. They're thinking about what we're asking them to do.

It is also interesting that the notion of negotiation had extended beyond the school, to include parents and their views of what happened in the school. Shirley Price recounted an amusing example of this, which I recorded in my field notes:

> Mrs Price recalls an amusing example relating to negotiation, which demonstrates that parents have also become knowledgeable about the extent to which negotiation is regarded as important. This concerns a pupil who was entered for two restricted grade Associated Examining Board (AEB) GCSE examinations. The pupil passed both examinations but later discovered the need for a higher grade GCSE qualification for entry to a particular course in FE. His father came to the school, to see Mrs Price in an attempt to persuade her to trade the two AEB basic passes for one higher grade GCSE. When she explained that this wasn't possible he replied, 'Well I thought you negotiated things in this school so what about this?' Mrs Price had some difficulty in making the parent understand that external examination grades were not left to her discretion.

Although an isolated incident which is unlikely to be typical of parents' actions in general, it does, nevertheless, illustrate the extent to which the identification of the school with the concept and act of negotiation had developed. The use of the term in everyday language and conversations around the school, the encouragement for pupils to take an active part in the process of negotiation, together with its physical manifestation by means of the negotiation room, gave the concept and the process great significance.

Whilst some of the difficulties associated with negotiation have been highlighted in this chapter, both staff and pupils generally showed a positive attitude towards it. Most staff agreed that they were able to get to know their pupils in more detail, and that negotiation enhanced pupils' communication skills. The head and several members of staff would go much further and argue that the emphasis on negotiation had gone to the very heart of the teaching and learning process. For example, Alan Neville, an experienced English teacher, although having reservations about some aspects of the Record of Achievement, believed the emphasis on negotiation had made a great contribution to the way in which teachers viewed pupils, and the way in which pupils viewed the school and education in general. He stated:

> There is an understanding of the value of their own [the pupils'] personal assessment of themselves, the fact that teachers cannot just say 'This is what I think of you, like it or lump it'. It's got to come through the majority of the staff, it's got to be negotiated with the child, you can't put something down on their Record of Achievement that they haven't agreed, and I think that is good because the child gets a much sort of broader understanding of, the significance of his action, the significance of what he does in school.

Whilst this largely positive view of negotiation was evident in Benton School the emergence of a number of important issues in relation to the extent to which real teacher–pupil dialogue took place and whether the term 'negotiation' actually discouraged discussion where pupil and teacher were in agreement should not be forgotten. Rather than merely a semantic argument about the difference between negotiation and discussion, the data from Benton pupils revealed important questions about power and control of the Record of Achievement and the negotiation sessions in particular. The data in many cases indicate something of a gap between the rhetoric of collegiality and teacher–pupil equality which surrounded the negotiation sessions and the pupils' experience of the sessions.

The evidence illustrates that invariably it was the teacher who remained in control of the negotiation process by deciding what the topics of discussion were to be, how long discussion would last and the extent to which the issues were negotiable. In this sense, the Record of Achievement process would appear not to have challenged the traditional teacher–pupil relationships to any great extent. Nevertheless, the very fact that negotiation sessions and the

Record of Achievement process existed was believed by some staff to affect their role as a teacher. Some teachers saw this as a potential challenge to their position and to their authority to which they had to respond. The following chapter will explore the extent to which the experience of the Record of Achievement process substantiated that belief.

4

CHALLENGING THE TEACHERS

You see, all this business of negotiating with children in Records of Achievement and changing your classroom practice to get out from behind your desk and amongst children, and putting yourself in, as they see it, a less secure position – it's very worrying to some traditional teachers.

(David Fox, headteacher)

The above quotations from an interview with David Fox shows quite clearly that although he was a great supporter of Records of Achievement and was keen to highlight their contribution to the school, he was also aware of some of the difficulties they might pose to teachers. In this instance, he was discussing the potential which Records of Achievement had for challenging the traditional role of the teacher. By fostering what is seen to be a more equal relationship between teachers and pupils by encouraging pupils to take greater responsibility for their own behaviour and learning, the role of the teacher may become less clear cut (cf. Meighan 1977; Phillips 1989). David Fox suggested, that by putting greater emphasis on the pupil, encouraging him/her to ask questions about the learning process, some of the security of the role of the teacher may be eroded. Indeed, as pupils take more responsibility for their own learning and progress through the process of negotiation sessions and goal setting it may be argued that the role of the teacher becomes somewhat ambiguous (cf. Evans 1989). For example, if the capacity for didactic teaching diminishes, does the teacher become more of a facilitator of learning, merely providing guidance to pupils when called upon to do so? Similarly, if (as David Fox would claim) pupil behaviour in the school has improved as a result of Records of Achievement, then it may be that the disciplinary aspect of the teacher's role has also been challenged or superseded by the Record of Achievement process.

Whilst such speculation may be taking things to the extreme, it serves to make the point that Records of Achievement may be powerful change agents where teacher–pupil relationships are concerned. Hargreaves *et al.* (1988) go so far as to call Records of Achievement a Trojan horse in this context. The case he puts forward is simple but effective.

> When thirty children tell you quietly and independently that they get very little from reading round the class, it is hard to resist the feeling that you really should do something about this. In this sense, profiles and Records of Achievement are a sort of Trojan horse.
>
> (p. 133)

By inviting pupils to comment on the way in which they are taught and encouraging them to see their own achievements in the context of the way the school is organized, the kinds of things they are asked to do and the style of individual teachers, the intention is surely to open up teaching and learning, to demystify its processes and to make it more of a partnership. In doing this, however, a challenge is posed to the teacher. A challenge to review his or her own practices, to evaluate and make changes where necessary.

Within Benton School the deputy, Pete Robbins, felt that some staff had experienced difficulty in opening themselves up to such challenges from their pupils. He explained:

> . . . their [the teachers] authority's challenged. I mean the old adage of this, you know, this teacher, this symbol, this mini god if you like, I mean that's got to go. I mean a lot of teachers can't, in common parlance, 'can't hack that at all'.

However, it may be that in this case Pete Robbins was putting forward an outmoded view of the classroom teacher. For example, many Benton teachers agreed that didactic methods had been in decline in the classroom for some time, not least due to the requirements of initiatives such as TVEI (cf. Gleeson 1987; Dale *et al.* 1990) and in particular the impact of GCSE (cf. Scott 1989). In this respect, Records of Achievement may be only one of the catalysts for change. Furthermore, whilst several teachers in the school believed their teaching styles to have changed, at least to some extent, due to the impact of Records of Achievement, and in this respect identified them as a challenge, few perceived that challenge to be a threat.

Moreover, some Benton teachers actively sought feedback from their pupils about the courses they taught, independently of the Record of Achievement. For example, George James issued a questionnaire to one of his science groups asking them to write a critical assessment of his performance. He was pleasantly surprised that pupils approached the task seriously, and although nobody was unduly critical of his performance he stated:

> Nobody made any horrible statements, so it doesn't bother me. No, but I'd listen if they were talking about criticizing the way I did a topic or taught a subject. I'd have some details first and then I'd see.

Providing pupils were able to substantiate their criticisms, this teacher felt 'challenges' from pupils could be valuable. He continued:

> . . . all of us have been on both sides of the fence, and we give it so why can't we take it? I don't see why they shouldn't. I mean if it's an outright stupid statement . . . well you just dismiss it, it's just irrelevant. What you're after is stuff you know, and [you] can see can help you.

Clearly, the approach of teachers who seek 'client validation' of this nature from their pupils differs substantially from the traditional role which sees the teacher as the focus of knowledge and authority and hence beyond questioning (cf. Burgess and Adams 1985). For George James, however, it was not the impact of Records of Achievement which had prompted this approach, but his own belief in the value of pupil evaluation.

The exposure of staff to critical comments from pupils in Benton

School was, therefore, not something which could be entirely attributed to Records of Achievement. Nevertheless, the issue of pupils challenging teachers during the Record of Achievement process in general and the negotiation sessions in particular, was discussed with Mavis Johnson, a fourth-year tutor quoted earlier, who provided an interesting perspective on the role of the teacher in these situations. Our conversation was as follows:

> CP: Do you ever feel as though you are being challenged by them; by the pupils? Taking those two boys as an example where they wouldn't agree on the statement, could that be seen as a challenge to your position as a teacher?
>
> MJ: No! Not me as a teacher, because I'm not really in the role of a teacher. I'm there as a negotiator and it's not me personally they're getting at, it's everybody in general.

For Mavis Johnson there was a clear distinction between her role as a classroom teacher and as a negotiator. Her interpretation of the negotiation role was sufficiently broad to enable her to absorb any criticism from pupils and to rationalize it in terms of being a representative of the staff and school as a whole. Whether taken consciously or not, this definition of her role in the negotiation sessions allowed Mavis to distance herself from any personal challenge brought by pupils. She continued:

> So it's not a challenge to me like it would be in the classroom if they decided to rebel. I mean that then is a very personal thing isn't it? As far as possible, I'm just a neutral person here.

What is interesting is that although all teachers stressed the need to get to know pupils well in order to engage in effective negotiation, Mavis saw her position as neutral. Given that the Record of Achievement process is about making decisions and about teachers and pupils making judgements, it is difficult to see how the form tutor, having the central role in the process, can be regarded as neutral. It appears that Mavis used what she described as her neutral position as a strategy to combat or absorb criticisms from the pupils.

All staff interviewed regarded criticism from pupils as something to be taken seriously. In more than one case, however, staff stressed that in order to be taken seriously there was a responsibility on pupils to provide honest and well-considered criticisms. The capacity of pupils to do so may be an issue for consideration. One member of staff explained that her approach to pupil criticism was always to ask pupils to provide supporting evidence. If she then accepted that they had a valid case, she was happy to discuss the matter with the pupil and look for ways of changing or improving it. She believed this could have a positive effect on teacher–pupil relations. She explained:

> I think it opens up the system. It sort of puts all the cards on the table a little bit more. It cuts down the barrier that's there.

It would seem, therefore, that as with the negotiation sessions, the Benton teachers were also in a position to 'control' or manage the criticisms and challenges which were made against them. They developed strategies to absorb the challenges. In this sense the power relationship again remained largely unchanged. Some changes in behaviour were encouraged by Records of Achievement on the part of teachers and pupils but enduring assumptions about status and power remained the same. Consequently, few teachers actually felt challenged or threatened by the Record of Achievement process, in the way that the deputy expected and they clearly did not see them as posing a serious threat to their position. This is not to imply that challenges did not occur, but rather that staff developed their own ways of coping with or using the challenges. Furthermore, the fact that staff had developed such strategies surely indicates that they remained in control not just of the Record of Achievement process and the negotiation sessions but also of the teaching and learning. Again the extent to which balance or equality between teacher and pupil was achieved, under such circumstances, may be questioned (cf. Philips 1989; Priestley 1990; Burgess *et al.* 1991). For example, the insistence that evidence be brought by a pupil to support a criticism, whilst seeming a reasonable demand for the teacher to make, again placed the pupil in a subservient position, being required to prove his or her case against the status and power of the teacher. Any discussion of the pupil's criticisms was not conducted, therefore, from a position of common esteem, but as with the negotiation session, from a position in which the pupil had everything to prove.

Teaching styles

A further area in which Records of Achievement may be seen to pose a challenge to teachers is in relation to teaching style. The decline of didactic teaching methods and the emphasis which Records of Achievement placed on pupil-centred learning necessitated a degree of self-evaluation in relation to teaching style for some Benton teachers.

Pete Robbins, the deputy head at Benton believed Records of Achievement to have been instrumental in bringing about changes in teaching style. During an interview at the start of the research he made the following comment:

> I believe a lot of teaching styles have changed. I know my teaching style has changed and changed for the better. I believe my teaching style was quite good before.

Personally, Pete Robbins has enjoyed good relations with pupils, and prided himself on his 'down to earth' approach to teaching. He gave as an example of this, his method for teaching mathematics:

> . . . you know we used to do what I call everyday maths . . . I'd sell a motorbike on HP you know, which to me is important because an awful lot of people get conned.

Although he stressed that he was able to adopt such an approach partly as a result of the good relationship he enjoyed with pupils, he realized that not all teachers were able to develop a positive rapport with their pupils. He believed, however, that such a rapport was important for a fruitful learning environment and in this regard, he believed that Records of Achievement had affected the way in which teachers approached their jobs. For example, he believed quite simply that the one-to-one pupil–teacher negotiation time allowed teachers to find out a great deal about their pupils. The kinds of things some pupils talked about may have been mundane or on the other hand spectacular, but the point was, they helped teachers to get to know their pupils. Pete Robbins explained:

> The things you talk about [may] be nothing to do with what you were negotiating, I would chat about them, you know, or say let's talk again about this. I think [the negotiation process] has helped an awful lot of teachers with their communication

problems with some of the young people, and I think it gives them another insight into some of the children.

He went on to recall a conversation with one pupil which he saw as instrumental in opening up their relationship and giving the pupil confidence to talk to teachers and to take a greater interest in his lessons. He recalled:

> One of the classic stories was of a lad who was not academic, he was not going to get anything at all from school academically, but we actually found out he was a cycling champion and once we knew that, he would come in on a Monday morning and I'd say, 'How did you get on at the weekend?' And all the so-called barriers were brought down.

In this case, the negotiation session provided teacher and pupil with something to talk about which was important to the pupil. It was also something in which he excelled. Pete Robbins believed that without the negotiation session the pupil's achievements would not have come to light and he would not have developed, at least socially, in the way that he did. Being able to talk about cycling from a position of knowledge and confidence gave the pupil status. More simply, it provided teacher and pupil with something to talk about and broke down some of the barriers which existed between them.

The data show, however, that attributing changes in teaching style directly to the impact of Records of Achievement is more problematic than the statements made by the deputy head perhaps imply. For example, a third-year tutor pointed out that differentiating between changes brought about by Records of Achievement and other initiatives can be difficult. She stated:

> It's very difficult because there are so many changes. You see I mean I didn't teach textiles I taught needlework and then suddenly it changed to textiles. So with the GCSE coming in and calling it textiles, and the Records of Achievement all coming in at once, everything has changed anyway.

Other members of staff, whilst not denying that changes had taken place in their teaching style, identified a variety of initiatives as important in enhancing change. Moreover, some teachers recognized that their teaching style had changed in recent years but were unable to attribute the changes to the impact of any initiative or development in particular. They saw their changes as part of a general change in the approach to teaching. For example, an interview with Paul Fryer, a maths teacher, revealed changes to a more pupil-centred, problem-solving approach to the subject, which may be seen to accord with the philosophy of Records of Achievement; but for this teacher, the impact of Records of Achievement had been minimal. The following excerpt from our interview illustrated this point:

> CP: . . . have you changed your teaching methods, teaching styles in any way to try and tease out those things that Records of Achievement look for?
> PF: No. I say no because literally my styles of teaching have changed in the last ten years radically.
> CP: Why is that?
> PF: Because I think maths is poorly taught, and needs to be taught in a different way to be effective. And the styles of teaching I prefer to use are those that are in the Record of Achievement.

For this teacher, Records of Achievement appear to have been accommodated by his teaching methods developed over the last ten years. They had not been the catalyst for change.

In general, most members of staff appeared to accept change as part of their role as a teacher. Many had been accustomed to change throughout their career; getting used to new approaches, new ideas was, therefore, part of the job. Phil Skelton, a fifth-year tutor, put forward this point of view in relation to teaching style:

> To be absolutely frank, I don't know that Records of Achievement have changed things enormously. I think it's having small changes . . . It's a broadening of perception possibly but I mean it's certainly not a massive change in direction of teaching style because of Records of Achievement. I mean again this is purely a pragmatic approach but I mean . . . that's the way teachers work.

Change was seen as something which was endemic. Records of Achievement were, in many cases, seen as just one more change in the role of the teacher and the job of teaching.

Nevertheless, there was an expectation within the school that teachers would need to change their teaching styles in order to accommodate Records of Achievement. A conversation with an English teacher, with many years' experience, revealed that requests had been made by the head that such changes should occur. Specific changes had not been prescribed but changes in general approach had been discussed. The English teacher declared, however, that for him, making the changes was difficult. He stated:

> *Teacher*: The only thing that's influenced the way I teach my subject is GCSE. And well the head's asked us to change the way we teach, to take in the new changes, Records of Achievement, etc. I haven't done it because, well, I teach the way I teach.
>
> *CP*: What sort of things has he recommended that you change?
>
> *Teacher*: He hasn't recommended anything, he just said, 'You know this whole approach to Records of Achievement can sort of change the way we teach in school, it can be that far reaching', which is what I might call a broad statement. But I need more specifics, maybe I'm not intelligent enough to see how it can be related.

For this experienced teacher who was not averse to trying new teaching methods, Records of Achievement had not proved to be the change agent in the same sense as GCSE; or, it would appear, to the extent that the head anticipated.

Some teachers, on the other hand, did identify Records of Achievement as instrumental in bringing change to their teaching style and their approach to the task of teaching. Some of the strongest exponents of this view were those teachers whose main subject base was thought to lend itself more readily than others to the philosophy and associated practices of Records of Achievement. Janet Fitch, an Art and Design teacher put forward a very positive view of the effect which Records of Achievement had on her teaching style. She stated:

> So I think the first thing it did [i.e. involvement in Records of Achievement] for me was to reassess the way I actually taught my subject.

After this, she explained that the nature of her subject helped in the active learning approach required by Records of Achievement. She continued:

> . . . having said that, my subject was already experience based learning . . . So I already, if you want, had a head start . . . I already treated all the pupils as individuals with their own specific needs and you have to in art and design, otherwise how would you assess where they're all at . . . but I think what the document did and what the process did for me was help me organize the results of that, if you like.

The nature of her subject meant Janet was accustomed to dealing with the individual needs of pupils. Furthermore, she was a popular teacher to whom pupils were able to relate and establish a rapport. Evidence of this may be seen from the fact that pupils had voted her chairperson of the School Council. Her ability for effective communication with the pupils also seemed likely to have contributed to the way in which she was able to integrate Records of Achievement with her teaching style. For her, Records of Achievement were not threatening and were easily accommodated in her approach to teaching.

The nature of the subject and its relationship to Records of Achievement was also discussed by Ken Gilbert, a Craft, Design and Technology teacher. He stated:

> I think that [giving attention to qualities specified by the descriptors] comes in to your overall assessment, no I mean, a lot of that is your skill as a teacher. And I mean we are used to being in an active learning situation, so we're used to seeing pupils in a number of different roles and a number of different situations. So I guess in this area [i.e. CDT] we are used to assessing them in that light.

For this teacher, Records of Achievement had been concerned primarily with changes in approaches to assessment rather than to teaching style. Like the Art teacher, his subject had always demanded a pupil-centred approach. Changes to teaching style had not, therefore, been dramatic. The subject base allowed an integration of existing teaching method with new assessment and reporting systems. It had not required massive changes in approach.

In general, Records of Achievement appeared not to have brought about massive changes in teaching styles in Benton School. Whilst most staff had made some changes to their approach to and methods of teaching, few attributed such changes directly to the introduction of Records of Achievement alone. Most saw the changes as part of a general evolution of teaching style brought about by a variety of developments and initiatives including, for example, GCSE, TVEI and Records of Achievement. Whatever the impetus for the changes, staff demonstrated a high degree of flexibility and accommodation. None of the teachers felt that retrograde changes in teaching method and style had been brought about by Records of Achievement or the other initiatives. Most welcomed the changes, and some saw Records of Achievement as providing some kind of legitimization and verification for changes which they had affected on their own initiative. This is not to imply that all teachers were entirely happy with all the changes, but most showed a generally positive disposition towards them and the following quotation from an interview with Brian Shaw, a fifth-year tutor, is in many ways representative of a general staff view of changes in teaching style.

> There have been changes in teaching style but it's part of an overall pattern. I mean, I think the Record of Achievement has required that we think more about our way of assessing pupils' skills, yes. It used to be quite easy just to write a report on a slip of paper and give it to the form tutor. In some ways that was a bit too easy.

The experiences of the Benton teachers with regard to teaching style would not seem to fit, therefore, with statements made by the headteacher and his deputy about the challenge of Records of Achievement. Whilst the interviews with staff suggested that the demands of Records of Achievement were not significantly different from those of GCSE and TVEI and hence require few adaptions in terms of teaching style, an alternative view would be to suggest that Records of Achievement remained largely separate from teaching and the curriculum. Apart from the more practical subjects of Craft, Design and Technology and Art and Design, there was little to suggest that the notion of pupil-centred learning had made great demands on the way in which staff taught their subject.

Evidence from the Benton teachers, together with the emphasis on completing negotiation in required time slots, suggests that the principal emphasis was on the summative Records of Achievement or the Document of Record, rather than the formative process. One experienced teacher expressed his views of the Record of Achievement in the following manner.

> I mean, I see the value of Records of Achievements very much as far as employers are concerned. A summative profile or Record of Achievement when a child leaves school gives a much clearer indication of just who the employer is going to deal with than the old-style school report. There's no doubt whatever.

His views were generally supportive of Records of Achievement yet like many of his colleagues he saw their contribution to formative assessment processes as minimal. In this respect whilst they continued to contribute largely to summative reporting and assessment it was perhaps not surprising that Records of Achievement appeared to have had little direct impact on teaching styles in Benton School. Whilst some teachers identified Records of Achievement as important change agents in their approach to teaching, many more saw them merely as one component of the many changes which had affected the job of the classroom teacher in recent years.

5

HITTING THE TARGET

An integral element of many of the Record of Achievement schemes developed either by individual schools, consortias of LEAs (e.g. the Oxford Certificate of Educational Achievement (OCEA)) or examination groups (e.g. the Midland Examining Group) is an exercise or process directed towards the identification of individual pupil learning objectives. Commonly termed goal setting or target setting, the process is again aimed at pupils taking some responsibility for their own learning by identifying particular objectives, usually in conjunction with a teacher, towards which they would work during the forthcoming academic year. The rationale which underpins the goal setting process is one which assumes that by identifying specific targets which are important to him or her, the pupil will be motivated to work towards their achievement. In this respect it is important that goals or targets are meaningful to the pupil and attainable (Garforth and Macintosh 1986). Unless pupils can see the reason for such targets and are able to demonstrate that they have been achieved, then it seems likely that the goal setting process will be seen merely as another component of the teacher-managed Record of Achievement (Hall 1989).

Benton School was no exception to the many others which had

developed a Record of Achievement in that goal or target setting constituted an important part of the process. Similarly, like many of the other schemes, Benton included the identification of the pupil goals or targets as part of the pupil–teacher negotiation sessions. Like the negotiation sessions themselves, therefore, the goal-setting activities were influenced by the extent to which teacher and pupil could establish an effective rapport and talk openly about the needs of the pupil. The idea of goal setting was such that it would provide an opportunity for the pupil to enhance his or her achievements and should not be used in any punitive fashion by staff to ensure that pupils engaged in activities which were more important to the teacher than to the pupil.

The kinds of goals which Benton pupils identified covered a wide spectrum. Some identified goals which related to school work, for example, to improve their performance in maths or to make greater efforts with their homework were two examples of general targets identified by fourth-year pupils. More specifically, one fifth-year girl identified a specific number of French verbs which she intended to learn before the next time she met her tutor to discuss progress towards the goals. Meanwhile, a fifth-year boy identified a series of novels which he intended to read over the same period. All pupils were encouraged to identify three goals, though some only identified two and others identified four, not all of which had to be related to academic pursuits. In this respect, many pupils identified goals which related to out-of-school activities. For example, during her fourth year, one pupil had set out to achieve a specific grade at Judo, another had expressed an intention to join the Duke of Edinburgh's Award programme of her youth club. Examples from younger pupils included a third-year girl who decided to aim at giving more help to her mother with household chores, and a second-year boy whose target was to lose weight for the sake of his personal appearance and health.

The examples above all relate to pupils for whom the goal-setting process did not prove to be particularly difficult as each was able to identify targets which were personally meaningful and were thought to be realistic in the time available. However, not all pupils had such positive experiences of the goal-setting process and for some the identification of targets, which were both meaningful and realistic, was not easy. For example, Ken Gilbert, a second-year form tutor, explained that helping pupils to identify such goals could be hard work. He stated:

It can be extremely difficult to come up with realistic goals,
if you spend twenty minutes negotiating with a child, I mean,
really to know the profile and to set realistic goals for them
you've got to spend a lot of time analysing that profile.

Ken Gilbert's concern was that goals should not be identified in
isolation but should emerge from the profile of the pupil which
become evident during the negotiation session. In this respect goal
setting could be contextualized and directly related to the pupil's
interests and experiences. In the case of Ken Gilbert's second-year
tutor group this meant that agreed goals tended to relate to pupils'
own personal development rather than to academic subjects. He
explained:

Second-year goals are mostly to do with, well, in my tutor
group anyway, are to do with independence, looking after
themselves and responsibility and beginning to take a bit more
responsibility for themselves, growing up, maturing. That,
is the area that I look at mostly and I pay very little attention,
in actual fact, to academic situations.

Although goals set by these second years were clearly pupil centred
and related to their own personal development it would seem that
they had been steered towards the identification of particular kinds
of goals by their form tutor. For example, Ken Gilbert declared
'growing up, maturing. That, is the area that I look at mostly and
I pay very little attention in actual fact to academic situations'.
In this instance the teacher's influence in the goal setting process
was clear. The extent to which Ken Gilbert described what he
looked for and what he payed attention to, by the use of 'I' in the
above quotation, suggests that the identification of goals and targets
was probably influenced more by the teacher than the pupil. The
example is useful, therefore, in examining the question of the extent
to which pupils should be given a totally free hand in identifying
goals and targets. Particularly with younger pupils, as in the case
of Ken Gilbert's form, it may be that the teacher needed to take
a more active role in order to ensure that goals were realistic for
the time and resources available to the pupils and that they related
to their overall development.

In setting goals and targets, teachers might usefully ask themselves, to what extent the goals which are agreed upon are their

own or the pupils' and whether they remain meaningful to the pupils in spite of teacher intervention.

Partnership

As with other aspects of the Record of Achievement it may be appropriate to see the identification of targets and goals as part of the teacher–pupil partnership which is fostered through the negotiation sessions. Hargreaves *et al.* (1988) take the issue of partnership in this instance further and suggest that goals, or what he terms contracts, should make explicit the change which is required not only by the pupil, but also by the teacher in order to enhance the learning and/or personal development of the pupil. Like Hargreaves I encountered very few agreed goals or contracts which required change on the part of the teacher. In this context goal setting did not form part of a teacher–pupil partnership and rather than enabling pupils to take greater charge of their own learning it seemed to have greater potential as a means of manipulation (Hargreaves *et al.* 1988) as teachers sought to elicit certain kinds of behaviour from their pupils.

Nevertheless, the rationale for the goal setting process in Benton School was expressed by the head and staff in terms of formalizing and encouraging pupil development in a non-threatening way which was meaningful to the pupil. However, it is difficult to judge the extent to which the goal-setting element of the Record of Achievement process was successful in its aims (cf. PRAISE 1988). For example, it would seem likely that the extent to which pupils regarded their individual goals as important would have an impact on their commitment to their studies and would generally contribute to pupil development. Comments from some fifth years suggested that goal setting and their achievement was not attributed particular importance. For example, my conversation with Helen illustrated this:

CP: You also set goals don't you?
Helen: Yeah [laughter].
CP: Why do you laugh? What sort of goals did you set?
Helen: Mm . . . [hesitation] . . . I can't remember . . . [hesitation] . . . Um, one of them was for something

out of school, to, um, be on the management for
[name of a youth group to which she belongs].

CP: Right. What about school goals, did you put any of
those down?

Helen: Um, I can't remember.

Helen's response to my question about goal setting was typical of
many pupils who claimed to be unable to recall the kinds of goals
they had set. For Helen goal setting did not seem to be an important
part of the Record of Achievement process. Furthermore, an interview held with Anna, another fifth-year pupil, revealed that the
identified goals did not necessarily maintain importance in the
everyday process of schooling. Anna's main goal had been to
achieve a pass in GCSE Mathematics.

CP: Once you have set the goals do you think about them
very often?

Anna: At first, then I forget [laughter].

CP: So you don't sit in your lesson thinking Oh I've set this
as my goal? When you're in a maths lesson for example, do you think, I must pass this because it's my goal?

Anna: No, I hope to pass it anyway.

CP: So did having it as a goal make any difference?

Anna: Not really.

In Anna's case it would seem that the goal was so closely identified
with one of the overall aims of the fifth year that it had little independent effect on her motivation or development. Passing GCSE maths
was seen as important whether it was an identified goal or not.
Evidence from Helen and Anna suggests that rather than being
kept in mind and constantly referred to, goals tended to become
forgotten.

In addition to agreeing the series of goals or targets as part of
the negotiation sessions all pupils received an 'updating' session
with their form tutor at a later stage, usually 6–8 months after
initially setting the goals. The updating session was designed to
review progress towards achieving the goals and to discuss any
particular problems which may have arisen since the initial negotiation session. In this respect the updating session was designed to
encourage pupils to keep their goals in mind and to provide
another formal, albeit much shorter, opportunity for one-to-one

teacher–pupil contact. It also provided a time to consider whether the goals were in fact relevant to the pupil and whether he or she was likely to achieve them before the next full negotiation session. In the case of Helen, quoted above, she revealed that it also gave the teacher the chance to remind her formally of the agreed goals.

Overall the pupil interviews revealed that identification of goals was not always seen as important. For example, it became clear that, in some cases, little thought had been given to their identification either before or during the negotiation sessions. Consequently, some pupils claimed to have thought of goals on the spur of the moment, with little guidance from their form teacher. My interview with Louise highlighted this point:

> CP: During your negotiation session you set yourself goals or aims, don't you?
>
> *Louise*: Yes, I don't think that's very good, I don't think that's necessary.
>
> CP: Why not?
>
> *Louise*: I mean, in my fourth-year profile I sat there for about ten minutes trying to think of one goal, and [the teacher] would not leave me alone until I'd thought of one. He kept saying 'come on, just think of one, off the top of your head'. I mean, what's the point of that?

Louise raises an important point. What is the point of thinking of goals 'off the top of your head'? Whilst this was not the case with all pupils, Louise's experience does raise questions about the identification of goals which are relevant and meaningful to pupils. Her experience suggests that goals were required merely to complete the process. It also brings into question the place of goal setting as part of the negotiation sessions. Concern with adequate time for negotiation has already been discussed and it may be that the need to complete an agreed statement, to discuss individual descriptor statements and produce a computerized record of them, leave little time for comprehensive and meaningful discussion of goals and targets. In this respect, the bureaucratic nature of the negotiation sessions could be seen to act against a full discussion of targets and goals. As a consequence, some pupils set targets which were achieved without any effort whilst for others they proved to be far too ambitious. Alternatively, they set targets which were indistinguishable from the objectives of schooling and school lessons in general and hence did not really maintain any great significance as independent targets.

However, there were Benton pupils for whom goal setting had proved worth while and several of those who had been successful in setting and achieving their goals spoke about the process with an obvious sense of pride. In some cases pupils believed that achievement of a particular goal had enabled them, not only to demonstrate competence in that particular area, but also to show qualities of determination, independence, perseverance, planning and organization. Several pupils felt that employers would be impressed by these qualities. A comment from Hannah, a fifth-year pupil, encapsulated many of these issues which were also expressed by other fifth years. She remarked:

> You achieve goals. Let's say like in the fourth year quite a few of us put that we have agreed goals to be a prefect in the fifth year and then you write down that you've achieved that goal. And you write things down like if you are a member of the school council, things like that. It makes it look like you are interested in school so then you go out of school as a responsible person.

For this pupil the value of identifying and recording the achievement of specific goals was seen largely in summative terms and in this sense the process took on an instrumental objective. In Hannah's case, rather than contributing to her personal and educational development, the achievement of goals was an opportunity for her to demonstrate to people outside of school that she was 'a responsible person'. Many Benton pupils saw the principal purpose of goal setting in these terms and as such it would appear that there existed some disparity between the teachers' aspirations for goal setting and the actual role that they played in the Record of Achievement process. Instances where pupils identified target setting as intrinsically important to their educational development were rare. Much more common were comments similar to Hannah's where achievement of goals made pupils a more marketable commodity and hence attractive to employers (cf. Stronach 1989; Ashforth 1990; Pole 1990).

The social context of goals

The development of goals as a means of marketing pupils to employers raises a set of important questions in relation to the perceived and real rationale for goal or target setting. Most Benton staff saw goal setting as an opportunity for pupils to take greater responsibility for their learning, and hence for the goals to contribute to the educational and personal development of the pupil. Whilst this may have happened with some pupils, it would appear that the achievement of specific goals was used as a symbol of pupils' employability. In this sense, goal setting and achievement had two agendas. In the first instance there existed the pupil development agenda which related to the substantive content of the goals. For example, learning more French verbs, reading a specified number of novels. Secondly, there was the work-related agenda evidenced through the demonstration of such qualities as determination, reliability, the capacity to plan and operationalize and ultimately to achieve. On the one hand, it would seem that goal setting was promoted for its intrinsic value to pupils' educational development; whilst on the other, the pupils at least saw the principal outcome of the process in terms of extrinsic, instrumental values.

Whilst there appeared to be no reason why goal setting could not and should not fulfil both agendas, the work-related agenda is surely another aspect of what Stronach (1989) terms 'ipsative' achievement. His discussion of Records of Achievement as tools with which schools market their products, the pupils, may be seen to apply specifically to the goal-setting process. In Stronach's terms then, the goal setting and achievement process could be seen as a result of 1980s Britain which encouraged individualism, determination and achievement. The 'Go for it' culture would seem, therefore, to underpin at least one of the agendas for goal setting. To see the rationale for the process in purely educational terms would surely be to ignore the wider social context of goal setting. In short, goals provide part of the fit between schooling and employers' demands for young people (Pearson and Pike 1989).

Moreover, the emphasis which was put on certain kinds of goals in Benton School produced a hierarchy of the kinds of targets at which it was appropriate for pupils to aim. Appropriate targets weren't solely or mainly academic but seemed to relate to an implicit code of what were perceived to be appropriate activities for secondary modern school pupils. For example, apart from academic goals, sporting targets were frequently identified as appropriate. One pupil elected to increase his training programme for middle-distance running in order to be selected for the county athletics squad. Another pupil identified acquisition of the Gold Standard Swimming Award within six months as one of her targets. Both of these sporting activities were seen as appropriate for goals alongside others which focused on more personal or family orientated targets. By contrast, one girl recalled that her tutor rejected her suggestion that winning a prize in a forthcoming disco-dancing competition could constitute a target. Similarly, another pupil who had found difficulty in identifying goals was advised not to include enhancing his beer-mat collection as one of his targets.

The identification of appropriate and inappropriate goals by staff may have served not only to distance the pupil from the process which was designed ostensibly to give him or her greater personal responsibility for learning, but also to apply values to different kinds of achievement. Collecting beer mats and disco dancing were deemed to be of lesser value, either intrinsically or in terms of their appeal to potential users of the Record of Achievement, than were athletics and swimming. What was called into question in these instances was not the capacity of the activities to demonstrate qualities such as determination, enthusiasm and independence, but the social connotations of the activities. In this respect there existed a social hierarchy of appropriate and inappropriate goals. The hierarchy in this instance was defined by the values of the teachers and their thoughts about what employers would regard as worthwhile achievements.

Does it make any difference?

Underpinning issues which relate to the rationale and function of goal setting is the question of whether or not it actually makes any difference to pupils. Whilst many claims have been made about the importance of target setting to the Record of Achievement process (Garforth and Macintosh 1986; Hitchcock 1986a; Law 1988) the effect that this process has in terms of enhancing pupil achievement is difficult to determine. The evidence from Benton

School suggests that pupils did not give great attention to their identified goals throughout the school year. My interviews with pupils revealed many who were unable to recall their goals and others who regarded their achievement as insignificant. In the main, pupils saw target setting as an isolated event which formed part of their negotiation session and as such was not something to which they attributed great importance. The reason for this may have been partly due to the system of reviewing and updating the goals. Procedures for this seemed to vary considerably between tutor groups. For example, some pupils recalled regular 'updating' sessions with their tutors where progress towards agreed goals was discussed, others said they had only discussed goals during their annual negotiation sessions, and some claimed never to have discussed them after they had been agreed.

Garforth and Macintosh (1986) suggest that one means of maximizing the effectiveness of target setting in relation to pupils' academic achievement is to link individual goals to the assessment and learning process in general. To identify effective and attainable goals, they suggest that school departments may need to examine critically what students should learn in order to identify those goals which should be achieved by all students and those which may be achieved only by some. Although Garforth and Macintosh are concerned essentially with achievement of academic goals, their general approach may be useful in identifying ways in which goal setting might be integrated with the overall learning and development of the pupil. From the experiences of Benton pupils, it would seem that in many cases, goal and target setting failed to have the impact that might have been expected because of a lack of opportunity for interim review. Consequently, goal and target setting became somewhat isolated events for many pupils, rather than part of a recording and reviewing process.

Garforth and Macintosh (1986: 37) offer a model for goal setting which has been developed below (Fig. 1) to place greater emphasis on the process of review and to portray an ongoing procedure which will continue as the pupil progresses between school years. The emphasis given to reviewing the goals acts to integrate the goal setting and achievement process with day-to-day school activities. In this way goal setting ceases to be an isolated annual event. If attempts were to be made to improve goal setting by

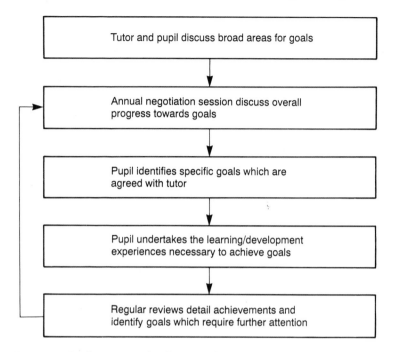

Figure 1 Goal setting: a developmental process.
Source: Adapted from Garforth and Macintosh (1986: 37).

emphasizing the process in Benton School, then ways for increasing opportunities for interim review would need to be devised. Figure 1 provides an example of one such opportunity.

Whilst Figure 1 attempts to formalize the goal setting and review process somewhat, it does not seek to apply a strait-jacket to it. The intention is to emphasize that goal setting and review is a dynamic process. If integration with teaching and learning is to occur, then the process should not be seen to have a beginning or an end, but should be ongoing.

In Benton School procedures for the reviewing and integration of goals with other classroom objectives had been only loosely devised. In this instance a lack of structure to the process meant that pupils were allowed to forget their goals quite easily or to see them as relevant only to the negotiation session. Figure 1 seeks to provide a structure for the process and by so doing enhance the contribution which it will make to the achievements of the pupil.

Ultimately the capacity of the goal-setting process to contribute to the development of pupils may depend on the importance attached to it by pupils and staff. The procedure detailed above may serve to attribute goal setting and the Record of Achievement process greater status by enhancing their contribution to pupil progress.

6

WHAT'S THE USE?

Discussion of the Record of Achievement so far has concentrated largely on issues concerned with its completion and with its contribution to enhancing pupil achievement, self-esteem and motivation. In short, discussion has been about administrative and organizational aspects of the Record of Achievement process and about its capacity to make a formative contribution to the development of the pupil. In considering the uses to which Records of Achievement may be put, however, it is also important to consider the summative role of the Record of Achievement.

In this chapter the two principal groups of Records of Achievement users are identified as parents and employers or institutions of further education to which pupils may transfer after their fifth year. However, to identify parents and employers as the main users of Records of Achievement is not to imply that they have the same needs with regard to information provided by the Record of Achievement. Clearly, parents and employers require information for different reasons; parents in order to know how their children are performing in school and employers to make judgements on whether the pupil should be offered a job or not. Although these two different needs exist and in order to meet them there is probably a requirement for different kinds of information, in Benton School the Summative Document of Record provided information in exactly the same form for both. This chapter will consider the Summative Document of Record in relation to its function as provider of information for parents and for employers.

Part of the rationale for the introduction of Records of Achievement in Benton School was that they would provide parents with a more complete picture of their child's school achievements. Consequently, the decision to adopt the Record of Achievement as the principal vehicle for assessment and reporting incorporated a decision to radically change the reporting system to parents. Early on in the development of Records of Achievement in Benton, the decision was made to abandon traditional subject-based reports which were issued once or twice a year (depending on the age of the pupil) in favour of a copy of the Record of Achievement which was to be sent to parents once a year.

In a letter to parents of second-year pupils the head introduced Records of Achievement in the following terms:

> This document [the Record of Achievement] completely replaces the traditional school report and should prove to be a more complete and thorough record of the achievements and standards of your son/daughter.

Furthermore, the Record of Achievement also sought greater participation from parents in the process of its production. Again as the head's letter explained, parents could give help to their children when completing certain pages of the Record. They were also asked to verify statements made by their children relating to activities about the home, and were themselves asked to complete a comprehensive list of questions which accompanied their child's Record of Achievement. As we have seen, the school took the view that as Records of Achievement sought to provide a more comprehensive picture of the pupil, it was relevant to include information relating to home-based activities, together with comments from parents. Both the head and the deputy, together with many teachers, argued that by collecting information about problems or concerns which parents had about their children, they are able to take a more holistic view of the pupil. As a result, they would be able to take action, to intervene, to provide encouragement or discuss issues with parents if necessary.

Numerous examples were provided by the head and staff of information gained from the parents' pages (Appendix 2) of the Record of Achievement which enabled them to take such action and bring about changes and improvements in pupils' behaviour or home circumstances. In particular, issues relating to personal relationships within families were highlighted. Changes in family circumstances (material and marital) were noted and the school had been able to take action or provide care which helped the situation. The head was particularly enthusiastic about the contribution which Records of Achievement had made to relations between the school and parents in this respect. This alone, he believed, provided vindication for the decision to abandon traditional school reports. He declared:

> That's a real bonus for me seeing more parental support and I'm sure that has something to do with the fact that we're inviting comments from parents in a more constructive way. We've highlighted all sorts of minor problems through the scheme between pupils and other agencies, or teachers or at home, that we've been able to deal with, that I'm sure would have become much more serious had we not gone through this process. We know a lot more about the children than we ever knew before.

Clearly, for the head, Records of Achievement were a useful tool not only for communicating with parents but also for facilitating intervention when necessary. The incorporation of parents into the process enabled the school to gather more information on their pupils, for a more complete picture of the individual to be produced, which enabled school achievements or concerns and problems to be viewed in a wider social/pastoral context. If, as the head believed, Records of Achievement were successful in achieving these things, then it is likely that they have a far greater formative impact on the process of schooling than traditional school reports ever could (Goacher and Reid 1984).

Care or surveillance?

Throughout the school, there was a general opinion that the involvement of parents in the reporting process had made a positive contribution to the level of pastoral care which the school was able to offer. However, the integration of the Record of Achievement and pastoral care systems raises a number of important questions concerning the collection and possession of information about individuals. For example, Hargreaves *et al.* (1988) raise important questions about the extent to which Records of Achievement could act as instruments of surveillance in this context. Their concern is that information collected for Record of Achievement purposes seemingly for pastoral reasons has the potential to be used as a form of social control against pupils. They state:

> . . . there are times when this proper concern can be extended so far as to amount to an unnecessary invasion of privacy. There is a similar side to the fact that pupils are open to assessment wherever they go. Whatever they do; that there is no space or activity which is protected from the teacher's surveillance.

> (p. 155)

The issue, therefore, is not merely the amount of information which is collected but the nature of that information which may relate to emotions and feelings as well as details about family life.

Hargreaves *et al.* (1988) drew attention to a section of the Warwickshire Record of Achievement which collected detailed information on pupils' home life. This section entitled 'Out of school' was employed in Benton for second- and third-year pupils. It asked them to indicate which of the following statements were true:

5.0 Out of school   Yes Sometimes No
5.1 You manage to get yourself up in   (tick one)
    good time
    You need a lot of calling and then
    have to rush around
5.2 You make your bed and leave your
    room tidy
5.3 You help with:
        Washing up
        Cleaning jobs
        Repair jobs
        Family wash
        Shopping

Cooking meals   Yes   Sometimes   No
Gardening

5.4 You have prepared a full meal
for yourself
You have cooked yourself a hot snack
You make a good cup of tea or coffee

5.5 You plan very carefully over a period
what you want to do with all
your money
You may plan to buy something
special, but you are usually quite
casual with money
You spend your money as soon as
you get it

5.6 You always get your homework done
without needing to be told
You have to be nagged to get down
to your homework
You'll do anything to avoid your
homework

5.7 When staying away from home:
You prefer to be with your family
You prefer to be with a group of
other young people

5.8 If you give your word that you'll do
something, you always do it
You always mean to keep promises,
but you sometimes don't carry
them out
You often forget to do things
you've promised

Although seemingly innocent, the questions provided personal information about pupils' family circumstances and gave insight into relationships with parents. The collection of such information from young pupils could surely be seen as an unnecessary invasion of individual and family privacy. Benton teachers could only justify its collection in general terms, referring to the need for information about 'the whole child' or insisting that details collected about the home and family enabled them to place school activities, achievements and behaviour in a wider social context.

Information about a pupils' bed-making activities and willingness to help with family washing or gardening may provide a more holistic picture but it is difficult to see its direct relevance to school-based formative development, or to pastoral care, or how it went beyond being plain nosy. Although the information collected might be perceived as mundane and not worthy of serious concern, it is the question of the reason for collecting information and the capacity for that information to be used for the good of the pupil which is the important issue. Benton teachers could provide no constructive suggestions for use of the information on bed making, room tidying, gardening and the like. Whilst their intentions were no doubt genuine the collection of such information provided an example of the capacity of some Records of Achievement to collect information on pupils which is neither useful nor relevant. In the context of pastoral care it gives rise to questions of the role of such information as a means of surveillance, not just of pupils but also of their families.

Moreover, the issue of social control through the Record of Achievement must be allied to storage and ownership of information. Whilst national policy makers (RANSC, 1989) made clear that the ownership of Record of Achievement data rests with the pupil and hence access to that information may only be granted by the pupil, the use of computers for the collection and storage of such information makes its transfer and reproduction easy (Pole 1991). The pupils' capacity to control access to Records of Achievement data seems likely to be seriously diminished once paper records are replaced by computers. In this context, any school storing pupil data on computer surely has a duty to inform its pupils of their rights under the Data Protection Act.

Reporting to parents

Amongst Benton staff, opinion was divided as to whether Records of Achievement were a more effective means of providing parents with information about their children than were traditional school reports. As traditional reports were abandoned upon the introduction of Records of Achievement a group of staff felt there had been insufficient time to evaluate the merits of Records of Achievement over traditional reports. Feelings on this issue tended to run quite high and were concerned not only with the amount of information rendered by the two instruments, but also their substantive content and scope. Needless to say, the head and deputy head were convinced that Records of Achievement were far superior to reports in the level of detail which they conveyed to parents. Consequently, it was their view that the introduction and development of a comprehensive Record of Achievement programme made the traditional report redundant. This was clearly the line taken at the time of the introduction of the Record of Achievement.

As we have seen, the extra time required for Records of Achievement was couched in terms of a trade-off with the time saved on the completion of traditional reports twice a year. However, a number of staff did not regard time as the main issue in this context and so remained sceptical of what Records of Achievement could offer which was not already provided by school reports. Others went further and suggested that the Record of Achievement's neglect of particular areas of assessment made them a retrograde step. Alan Neville, for example, regretted the fact that the Benton Record of Achievement did not include comments from teachers about pupils' performance in particular lessons. He believed such comments to be valued by parents, above information relating to the character and behaviour of their children. He asserted that parents already knew about those kinds of things, and it was teachers' opinions of pupils' performance in lessons which was particularly important. He stated:

> I mean, they [parents] know whether their child is cheerful, or they know whether their child can persevere, they know this and the other about the child, they don't need, really, the school to tell them. What the parents want to know is, they want to know what the teachers as people, think of their children.

In Alan Neville's opinion, Records of Achievement focused on the wrong kind of information for parents. His statement is important in that it draws attention to the difference between qualities and specific skill-based achievements. The Benton Record of Achievement with its concern for general issues such as cheerfulness, perseverance, communication and ability to work with others, for example, neglected to report on specific skills and achievements which were subject related. This concern is one which underpins a fundamental criticism of the Benton descriptor statements which sees their treatment of qualities and skills as largely the same, in terms of their capacity to be learnt and demonstrated by pupils, as incorrect and misleading. Alan Neville's point is that qualities such as cheerfulness and perseverance cannot be taught but are part of human nature. By contrast skills like literacy, numeracy, an ability to conduct scientific experiments or play a musical instrument can be taught. To confuse qualities and skills is, therefore, to confuse the whole issue of achievement. Clearly, the argument has serious implications, not only in terms of reporting to parents but also in terms of the capacity of the descriptor-led process to contribute to the formative Record of Achievement process and ultimately to the development of the pupil. This is not to imply, however, that he saw no role for Records of Achievement. On the contrary, he believed that they had an important summative role to play with employers.

Nevertheless, due to the omission of teacher comments and subject specific information, Alan Neville declared:

> I don't think personally that Records of Achievement are as good for parents as school reports.

He supported this view of the failure of Records of Achievement with anecdotes of complaints from parents about the lack of teacher comment on the Record of Achievement. He recalled:

> . . . their reactions were frequently 'Why can't teachers make comments?' . . . they wanted comments from the teachers.

Whilst Alan Neville probably put forward an extreme view of what he saw as the failure of Records of Achievement, other members of staff expressed similar concerns about the absence of teacher comment. For example, Paul Fryer, a fifth-year tutor, was concerned that the absence of teacher comments on the Record of Achievement removed an opportunity for formative reporting. He stated:

> Well, I think one of the things that is missing from Records of Achievement, but is on reports, is a sort of form, when you are writing a report, you have a form saying how Johnny's doing, but I always used to write what Johnny needed

to concentrate on to improve himself in that level. That's gone now hasn't it and I think that's one part of communication that has disappeared because of Records of Achievement but to me it was very important and important to parents.

This view was echoed by a considerable minority of staff who felt they were being denied the opportunity to point out to parents exactly where more attention could be given in particular subject areas in order that pupils might improve their performance. It is interesting that Paul Fryer should interpret the failure of Records of Achievement to do this as a failure in communication. Given that part of the rationale for the introduction of Records of Achievement (DES 1984) was that they would engender more effective communication with parents, claims that they actually reduce the level of communication must be taken seriously. Moreover, Paul Fryer's claim that they precluded opportunities for formative reporting which had the capacity to enhance pupil performance in particular subject areas would also seem to run counter to one of the four main aims of Records of Achievement (DES 1984).

The absence of subject-specific comments from the Record of Achievement was frequently discussed amongst the staff, several of whom made their concerns clear to the head. During an interview I conducted with him he defended their absence in the following terms:

> I don't see this as a serious problem, personally, I think the internal examination statement the parents get, the parent/ staff evening where they can talk subject specific and the indicator on Records of Achievement up to and including the fourth year of their attainment in effort areas in every subject area, I think that's sufficient you see.

Clearly, David Fox regarded the various statements which parents received by way of the Record of Achievement as informative. Should further information be required, this could be gained from parents' evenings or by arranging to see a member of staff. In this context he saw the Record of Achievement as a starting point for conversation between teacher and parent at a parents' evening or a requested meeting.

Furthermore, evidence from two fifth-year pupils, David and

Paul, suggested that Records of Achievement were working in the way intended by the head. Our conversation brought this to light.

CP: What do your parents think of the Record of Achievement?

David: They're quite pleased, 'cause they are actually getting to see what's happening about their son, and they feel they've got an active part in it.

CP: What about yours, Paul?

Paul: Yeah, mine feel the same way. The parents' page especially, my Dad likes to fill that in and likes to keep in touch with the school and see how I'm getting on and when they come down for parents' evening they get to talk to the teachers. So if you're not doing enough work at school, or doing enough work at home, they can put that right, easily.

However, not all staff accepted the Record of Achievement as a facilitator of conversation and there was a feeling that it lacked the necessary precision required of a reporting document. For example, one teacher expressed quite strongly a concern that factual information was largely missing from the Record of Achievement. He saw this omission as inevitable whilst the Record of Achievement process relied upon an aggregation of teacher opinion. Consequently, he saw the information presented to parents as wholly unsatisfactory. He stated:

> They [parents] don't know what their [child's] position is, or their estimated grade is or anything like that unless they get told, even the exam entry form doesn't tell them that. So I don't know, they don't give certain factual information, they give a mishmash because everybody inputs into it, you know and you come to a solution which is if you like, agreed by everybody, in other words it's not strong opinion, it's middle of the road opinion.

These comments raise the important issue of objectivity in reporting. For this teacher, Records of Achievement did not offer sufficient precision and were based merely on the opinions of a number of teachers. They lacked the rigour of reporting systems which were based on pupil performance in individual subjects and as such failed to offer parents a clear picture of their child's performance.

However, the fact that Records of Achievement were the result of a process of discussion between teacher and pupil and precisely because they were based on comments from a number of teachers led the head to argue that they offered a kind of objectivity which was not possible with traditional school reports. The opposing views of Alan Neville and David Fox came to light in a heated discussion which I witnessed in the latter's office. I recorded the conversation in my field notes in the following way:

> There then followed a conversation between Mr Neville and Mr Fox about the merits of Records of Achievement in relation to the information they provide for parents. Mr Neville maintained that they fail to give parents what they want in so far as they do not include comments from subject teachers. Mr Fox defended this position very strongly by insisting that such comments were not appropriate because they were entirely judgemental and not at all objective. Mr Fox sees the Records of Achievement process and the negotiation process as an objective exercise. He also sees agreement between pupils and staff as objective. He feels the inclusion of what he sees as a totally subjective teacher comment, would go right against the philosophy of the Record of Achievement. Mr Neville maintained that parents want to know how their children are performing in particular subjects, and the Record of Achievement, as it stands, does not provide this kind of information.

The conversation is important in highlighting the issue of the possible uses to which Records of Achievement might be put and the audiences they might address. Alan Neville's concern related to the capacity of Records of Achievement to fulfil a formative function. In his opinion the records failed to do this as they were largely subjective and could not offer a sound foundation upon which to base further developments. As such, their main role was in summative reporting to employers and institutions of further education. Whilst David Fox also identified an important summative role for Records of Achievement, he clearly believed they had an important formative role. Furthermore, he saw this formative role as particularly strong given that development could be based on the objective information contained within the Records.

The debate about formative and summative reporting is clearly one which has been central to the development of Records of

Achievement (Broadfoot 1986; PRAISE 1988; Hall 1989; Munby 1989). In Benton School the debate took on a particular intensity in the light of traditional school reports being abandoned. The Record of Achievement was required to act as a summative report to parents each year and as the basis for improving pupil performance in school over the coming year. The extent to which these two different roles could be met by one document remained a cause for concern amongst the staff. Those who questioned the capacity of the Record of Achievement to provide adequate information to parents seemed not to be concerned with the inadequacies of the Record of Achievement but with the demise of the traditional school report. However, those who held this view tended to be the older members of staff and it may be argued that they shared a somewhat idealized and uncritical view of school reports (cf. Ryrie *et al.* 1979; Goacher and Reid 1984).

Overall, the majority of Benton teachers had no regrets about the demise of traditional reports which were seen to be short on detail, not least because of their physical layout which offered very little space for comments to be entered. As a result, very general statements tended to be made which provided little in terms of contextual explanation or in terms of links between and across a number of subjects. Furthermore, some teachers recalled using the same stock of comments each year and distributing these throughout their classes. Moreover, several teachers made reference to pupil self-assessment which was encouraged as part of the Record of Achievement process. They believed this, allied to target setting, had the potential to contribute to pupils taking greater responsibility for their own learning and hence for their own personal development. Traditional summative reports clearly were unable to make such a contribution to pupil development.

In relation to this the process necessitated by Records of Achievement was also welcomed by staff who saw the 'snapshot' provided by the traditional report as inadequate. The Record of Achievement enabled a more complete picture of the pupil to be formed which could take account of performance and progress over the school year, and contribute to improvement and development. The traditional report was often seen by staff as a static document which could offer little in terms of development of the pupil. Brian Shaw, a fifth-year tutor, believed the developmental aspect of the Record of Achievement, through the participation of the pupil, gave it a fundamental advantage over the traditional reporting system. He stated:

> *BS:* . . . One of the fundamental differences between this system and the previous report system . . . is that pupils have . . . an input which matters. In other words, one of the complaints that's often been levelled at the traditional reporting system by pupils, not so much by parents, but by pupils themselves, is that they didn't have a say in what was said about them.
>
> *CP:* So all they got was what was written in their report at the end of term?
>
> *BS:* What the staff thought about them sort of thing. Whereas now they understand . . . that they have a part to play in the process, that their point of view matters, which I think was never the case with the traditional reporting system. A lot of what we do in teaching, certainly at this level, is about making pupils feel involved in what they are doing.

Brian Shaw was typical of many Benton teachers, in his perception of the Record of Achievement as something more than a reporting device for parents. Rather than something which is merely a report on the pupil, the Record of Achievement is a process, in which the pupil is a major contributor. However, the extent to which this was the case for all pupils in Benton School and schools elsewhere should be examined in the light of comments made earlier about control and negotiation.

However, whilst Records of Achievement and traditional reports are frequently compared with each other, the significant differences between them in terms of the aims, content, process and structure, renders such comparisons meaningless. To view the Record of Achievement merely as a reporting device for parents would be to disregard many of its functions, aims and objectives. It would also be to disregard the philosophy of formative recording and assessment which is fundamental to Records of Achievement.

Parents' responses

Having argued that direct comparisons between Records of Achievement and traditional school reports are largely pointless, it was nevertheless the case that in Benton School both methods had been used to report on pupil progress. It did not seem unreasonable, therefore, that staff, pupils and parents should seek to make such comparisons. The school report, for many parents, was the principal link between the home and the school. For some, it may have been the only link. Furthermore, the fact that school reports have remained basically the same in terms of format, content and style, for many years, makes them familiar documents to most parents (Goacher and Reid 1984). Many schools issue parents with summative reports which are essentially the same as those which would have been issued to their own parents many years before. There is, therefore, an important history attached to school reports which identifies them as an important part of schooling (Ryrie *et al.* 1979) and creates an expectation amongst parents for particular kinds of information about their children in a style with which they are familiar and which can be easily understood.

Given this tradition and history the significance of Benton School's decision to abandon school reports in favour of Records of Achievement, which were at that time largely untested new documents, should not be underestimated. The importance of this decision was recognized at the very early stages of the introduction of Records of Achievement in the school. Both the head and the deputy recalled parents' evenings which were held to introduce and explain Records of Achievement to parents. Supporting literature produced by the school was also sent out giving details of what was involved in the Record of Achievement process, and of the parents' role in it. The head remembered stressing to parents that Records of Achievement were a comprehensive method of formative assessment in which the role of parents, together with home life and out-of-school activities, was attributed great importance. Similar events were organized for parents of children who were new to the school, and explanations of the Record of Achievement process also formed an important part of its 'marketing strategy' when attempting to attract pupils from local middle schools. The head saw the support of parents as central to the success of Records of Achievement in the school. Consequently, he was prepared to spend considerable time discussing and explaining the process, the rationale and the various documents to them. He felt this paid off in the level of support parents had shown for

Records of Achievement, and in the positive comments which many had made about them.

As part of the reporting function of Records of Achievement, parents were invited to make written comments on the document which their children brought home. Considerable importance was attached to the parents' view of the Record of Achievement and of their reaction to its contents. Two sides of A4 were given over to parent comments. One side contained six questions (see Appendix 2) giving parents the opportunity to comment on their child's progress, on statements made by staff and their children in the Record of Achievement and to draw attention to any particular issues which they felt the school should be aware of. The second page gave parents the opportunity to expand on any issues which they felt relevant to the progress of their child. Altogether, the document sought much closer co-operation from parents in the reporting and recording process than traditional reports ever did or could.

The head claimed that very close to 100 per cent of all parents' pages were completed by parents and returned to the school. Furthermore, the number of additional detailed comments which were made on the forms was far higher than anything ever achieved through the system of traditional reports. Jackie Saunders, the Record of Achievement co-ordinator, was responsible for collecting the completed parents' pages and was able to quantify the level of response. She said:

> JS: I would think probably something like one-third of the parents just sign the papers and that's all you get. And the rest comment on various bits, and they're quite construc-tive comments.
> CP: What sort of percentage of returns are you getting?
> JS: Oh, we get all of them back.

The fact that all parents at least signed and returned their part of the Record of Achievement may be seen as an achievement in itself, and an indication that the school was able to communicate suc-cessfully with parents through the medium of the Record. The head claimed that this level of response had been largely unknown for anything other than Records of Achievement and in many cases was just a starting point for further communication between parents and the school. As Jackie Saunders explained.

> . . . when the Records of Achievement come back they come
> back to me and I go through them. Any comments that we
> ought to act on I pass on to Year heads . . . They will decide
> whether we need to send a letter home, need to have the
> parents in or whatever. For the most part we send a letter
> home and invite the parents to come in if they want to.

The parents' response to the Record of Achievement may, therefore,
prove to be a first step in the communication between home and
school. It may prove to be a useful tool for both the parents and the
school in identifying and taking action over issues relevant to the
progress and development of the pupil.

In addition to writing about the progress of their children, many
parents made comments about the Record of Achievement itself.
Although the head stressed that the overall tone of these comments
demonstrated a positive view of Records of Achievement from
parents, the issue of the absence of teacher comment was, nevertheless, raised. The following examples of parents' comments are
illustrative of those to which I was given access by the head:

- We think the 'Record of Achievement' is a very good idea,
  because it gives everyone concerned a say and we think it
  gives the teachers more idea of the character of the pupil and
  how they 'tick'.
  We believe Jenny has been very frank and honest in her
  comments and perhaps surprised us with her 'revelations'.
  She has very strong opinions on some matters, but we think
  her reluctance to express herself probably lies with the fact
  that she thinks others are entitled to their own opinions and
  she doesn't like to press hers strongly on other people. We
  think you will find that when she meets with a kindred spirit
  she will express her views quite strongly.
  All in all we are delighted with her progress, not only in the
  academic field, but in her own personal development. We
  hope she will carry this on through next year and reap the
  rewards she deserves.
                                                          Thank you.
- We hope that the Record of Achievement scheme proves
  to be a success. It would appear to be a much fairer assessment of a child's progress than a report which is based solely
  on examination results and written school work.

- We are quite impressed with 'Profiling' as a system of assessment as opposed to the conventional 'end of term report'. However, we have one main criticism, i.e. we are disappointed that there are virtually no constructive comments from teachers as to progress and although marks in Jane's case are good in the main, we feel that some comment (favourable or otherwise) would be of benefit to both pupil and parent.

- We feel this is a better way of assessing the child's progress and gives teachers, parents and pupils the chance to comment. I think perhaps the teachers could make more comment than they have.

- We welcome the profile concept and hope it will lead to a 'contract' between the staff and pupil to get the best out of school.

- There appears to be little that I can disagree with due to the lack of comments available on the section completed by the teachers. I feel her achievement grade in music does not reflect her true performance.

These comments are for the most part, supportive of Records of Achievement, with parents recognizing that they have a positive contribution to make to the development of their children. However, calls for more comments from subject teachers were common. In this respect it would appear that Records of Achievement were failing to meet one of the important needs of parents. Whilst the head and many members of staff would defend this position by pointing to the positive parent comments about the process of Records of Achievement, together with the inadequacies of traditional school reports, it may be argued that the Record of Achievement was failing in one of its principal aims; to be an effective summative document. Although the formative contribution to the process of schooling made by Records of Achievement was largely unchallenged by the parents, questions were posed about the suitability of one document to act both formatively and summatively. In this respect the tenor of the parents' views would seem to accord with those of Alan Neville and several other teachers who saw them as inadequate for the purposes of reporting to parents. Overall, parents' views were positive and many welcomed the opportunity to contribute to the reporting process by means of the parents' pages. Clearly, this is not to imply that all aspects of the Record of Achievement were accepted without question by parents and in some cases a degree of ambivalence existed. One teacher reflected on the overall parental reaction and attempted to characterize a degree of conflict which she had identified. She explained:

> I think there's a bit of a conflict from the parents' point of view. I can remember my form in the second year last year, and that was obviously the first time they'd come into contact with a Record of Achievement document and a lot of comments came back from parents, which said, 'Yes great, we love it, told us a lot about our child, a lot we already knew but we'd like more comments about the actual problems'. So I think you've got a problem here with parents who really would like an old style report and feel safer with that because it's listing down, exactly, if you like, what they need to clip a child round the ear over. I think there's a bit of a problem and I'm still getting parents now saying 'Yes, it's smashing and we like it, but we'd still like more comments from the staff'.

The conflict, as this teacher termed it, is illustrative of one of the difficulties associated with introducing change to a well-established reporting system. Parents were familiar with traditional reports, they knew what to expect and as this teacher asserted, they felt safe. These reactions are important, therefore, in reminding those responsible for the promotion of Records of Achievement that users who receive formative or summative records need to be educated in their use. In this case, parents would probably have benefited from greater explanation of the rationale and purpose of the Record of Achievement which emphasized both formative and summative roles. They might also have received some indication as to why teachers' comments about specific subjects were absent. Similar points can be made in relation to other potential users of the Records, in particular, employers and representatives of institutions of further education (cf. Ashforth 1990; Pole 1991).

Notwithstanding, the reservations which some parents expressed about the absence of teacher comment in the Record of Achievement, most agreed that the summative document, together with the formative process, proved to be helpful in highlighting difficulties and areas of concern with individual pupils where the school might usefully take some action. Furthermore, there was evidence from the returned comments that some parents welcomed the formal opportunity to raise issues of difficulty and concern with the school which the Record of Achievement afforded. The following extract from a parents' page illustrates the kind of issues that parents brought to the attention of the school through the medium of the Record of Achievement.

> We have been having some problems with Robert at home with regards to who he is mixing with and what he is getting up to out of the home. One boy in particular is not a very good influence and we have had to keep Robert in, mainly to keep him away from this other boy. One of the biggest problems we seem to have is that most of the boys in our village attend other schools now and have made other friends. At the moment we are trying to encourage Robert to see that it is foolish to hang around the village with a 'trouble maker', making a nuisance of himself to people. He is beginning to see the light, we think, and hope!
>
> We are hoping to see him taking part in more sporting activities after school, so that he is doing something interesting and positive. Also he can be using up some of his energy and possibly getting rid of some of his aggression.
>
> It is very easy to get to the point of despairing of Robert and recently we have been very close! However, he isn't really such a bad lad, and we think we may be able to help him make something of his life, if the right things are encouraged.

On receipt of these comments from what were obviously concerned parents, Benton teachers were able to take action in respect of encouraging Robert to take part in sport and to counsel him in relation to his choice of friends and associated out-of-school activities. The action the school took was condoned and supported by Robert's parents who were grateful for the interest shown by the head and the teachers.

Whilst it should be stressed that not all comments from parents referred to problems or difficulties with their children, members of staff believed that in Robert's, and several other cases, Records of Achievement gave them access to information which would not have been made available in any other way. Consequently, they were able to take appropriate action to assist or support the pupil.

In general, Records of Achievement appeared to act as a useful means of communicating with parents, and both the head and members of staff assured me that parental support for them was strong. The calls from parents for more teacher comment about specific subjects and the support for these calls which existed among the staff should not, however, be underestimated.

Reports for employers

Apart from parents those most likely to make frequent use of Records of Achievement are employers and their representatives (Andrews 1989; Ashforth 1990). Stronach (1989) argues that the rationale for the widescale introduction and development of Records of Achievement can be located in terms of the need for employers to have access to greater information about school leavers in order to facilitate effective recruitment. In these terms Records of Achievement may be seen simultaneously as a tool for employers in their recruitment practices, and as a form of marketing, both for individual school-leavers, and for the schools from which they are leaving. Viewed in this instrumental sense, Records of Achievement contribute to the wider debate about the relationship between education and industry. For example, Garforth and Macintosh (1986) have argued that one of the reasons for the development of Records of Achievement during the mid-1980s, relates to the disaffection of employers with the world of education.

The changes which have occurred in education in recent years – for example TVEI, GCSE, CPVE and the National Curriculum – have left many employers confused as to what school-leavers have to offer them. Records of Achievement provide a medium therefore, whereby employers are able to gain a clearer picture of their potential recruits. In this respect, Broadfoot (1982) argues that Records of Achievement tell us much more about an individual than examination results ever could, including information about their interests and the qualities of the individual. Furthermore, the fact that such information is expected to be of use to employers when selecting pupils may be seen from the joint launch of the National Record of Achievement by the DES and the Department of Employment (DES 1991).

Several teachers regarded the provision of information to employers as the main benefit which pupils could gain from Records of Achievement. On a national level, however, information relating to employers' responses to Records of Achievement remains scarce. That which does exist, however (cf. Andrews 1989; Ashforth 1990; Pole 1990) is favourable and suggests that when employers are given access to summative Records of Achievement they make constructive use of them. Moreover, conversations with David Fox indicated that on a local level those employers with whom Benton School had regular contact also found the Record of Achievement to be useful, to the extent that some were beginning to request that Benton pupils include copies of their Document of Record with any job application. In the view of the head, the Record of Achievement made an important contribution to the positive relationship which existed between Benton School and the local employing community.

However, the school's experience of using summative Records of Achievement with employers gave rise to a range of issues and questions. In particular these issues relate to the kind and amount of information to which employers were given access. In particular the exclusion of negative statements from summative documents, the willingness of school-leavers to use their Document of Record for recruitment purposes and the status of the Document *vis-à-vis* confidential references and traditional test and examination results.

The report of the Record of Achievement National Steering Committee (RANSC 1989) makes clear that all statements included in a summative Record of Achievement, the Document of Record, should be positive. As such, it may be useful to think of the Document of Record as a detailed curriculum vitae in so far as it is a résumé of accomplishments and achievements supported by an agreed statement jointly written by teacher and pupil. In its concern to celebrate the success of the individual, negative statement of failure to achieve are not deemed to be appropriate for inclusion. For some Benton staff, however, the omission of negative statements was seen to be problematic. For one teacher the absence of such statements caused him to question much of the Record of Achievement process, and its capacity to portray a complete picture of the pupil. During an interview he was anxious to make the following points:

> One of the main things that I'm against about this Record of Achievement, it really doesn't show negative statements. And, you know, if I was an employer I would like to see them, not on every statement, but just to get a clearer picture of that certain individual.

Although concern about negative statements was not common amongst the staff there was, nevertheless, a general feeling that Records of Achievement could result in the portrayal of a fairly standard picture of pupils, which failed to differentiate between high and low achievers. In this context, several teachers thought that the inclusion of negative statements would not only make it easier for employers and other users of the Document of Record to identify strengths and weaknesses in potential recruits, but it would also result in a more accurate reflection of achievement across the year group and avoid any standardization. There was also a feeling that without negative comments the Documents of Record would appear bland. Similarly, Nick Reilly, a third-year tutor, saw a difficulty in the summative Document of Record's failure to be precise. He remarked:

> . . . it doesn't give a very good overall picture. You know, its a bit from here and a bit from there, you pick out.

As a result of the 'picking out' Nick Reilly believed an aggregated picture was formed which said little about the individual pupil (cf. PRAISE 1988).

Phil Skelton, another teacher, who had taken some responsibility for developing the computerized descriptor banks from which summative statements were drawn, believed that the overall similarity amongst the Documents of Record could be attributed to the emphasis placed on the use of the descriptor banks. He recounted an experience which he felt made him well qualified to make such a criticism. He explained:

> So I actually sat in front of a printer for hours on end [the printer had broken and required paper to be fed in manually] watching these things [summative records] coming out and of course you get the stuff at the beginning and then you just get the same descriptors, you know and you get 50 kids with, apart from minor changes, nothing different.

If the summative documents produced by the Record of Achievement process are essentially bland, and show marked similarities with each other, then it may be pertinent to ask what exactly are employers and other users being presented with? How far are summative documents helpful in recruitment procedures, and ultimately to what extent are they helpful to pupils seeking to enter the labour market or further education?

The failure of the Document of Record to differentiate adequately between pupils raises questions about the capacity of the Record of Achievement to meet one of its fundamental aims of producing reports which are sensitive to the characteristics, achievements and experiences of the individual pupil. Hargreaves *et al.* (1988) suggest that the use of comment banks or descriptors may, to some extent, be responsible for taking away the individual pupil authorship of Records of Achievement and producing a standard profile which makes all pupils appear similar. If this is the case then there are important implications for the value of the summative Record of Achievement and the likely use that recruiters will make of it. As such, any improvements which Records of Achievement bring to summative reporting must be seen as relative rather than absolute. Whilst Phil Skelton's experience illustrates their failure to differentiate between pupils, the same must also be said of examination results and traditional school reports. However unless Records of Achievement can accommodate individuals by engaging with and representing their individuality then they may become nothing more than an opportunity for teachers and pupils to talk with each other. Whilst this in itself may be valuable it does not meet the basic aim of Records of Achievement to ' . . . provide a more rounded picture of candidates for jobs or courses than can be provided by a list of examination results . . .' (DES 1984).

Phil Skelton went on to suggest, however, that the principal means by which the Document of Record was able to differentiate between pupils was by the student summary statement (the section of the document which pupils write themselves and is concerned with their interests and activities in addition to their personal view of their achievement). He explained:

So, I mean, the ones that stood out were those who had, you know three-quarters of a page of A4 crammed into their personal statement. You know that they were members of this, and did that, and won cups for this you know, where as a lot would say 'I like watching Neighbours on the telly', you can draw your own conclusions. But that was the main area of distinction and I think one of the areas which might be interesting to explore, because you can say OK what's it trying to achieve as a summary document, summarising this person as a human being? And do we want it to discern? And to what extent is it succeeding?

Alan Neville, who also had experience of liaison with employers, took a different view from Phil Skelton. He was able to point to a precise example where differences between pupils were made very clear through the Record of Achievement. He explained:

I mean, I was at a careers briefing with some industrialists recently and I took along with me a Record of Achievement of a very good girl, and a Record of Achievement of a boy who wasn't so good and I just put them side by side and I said, you know, what do these tell you about these children? And she stuck out a mile as being brilliant, you know, the kind of person you'd want.

Alan Neville argued that Records of Achievement do have the capacity to differentiate between pupils and in doing so provide the employer with useful information. As he recalled his meeting with industrialists he highlighted a number of other issues relevant to employers' use of Records of Achievement. He continued:

. . . everything on his [the boy's] Record of Achievement was positive, it said lots of things about him, but the girl's was about six pages long, his was about three pages long, you know what I mean, and anyone who's worth their salt, any employer who's worth their salt and looks at the full list of descriptors, before they start interviewing people, based on Records of Achievement, knows what the full range is. Just by looking at it, they can tell which ones have been left out, that's the important point, which ones have been left out.

Whilst Alan Neville does not recall any concern expressed by employers over the length (six pages) of the girl's Record of Achievement, statements made by the Record of Achievement National

Steering Committee (RANSC 1989) and the Confederation of British Industry (CBI 1983) recommended that final summary documents should be brief, no more than three sides of A4. They hoped this would encourage users to read them in their entirety. To produce six sides of A4 may result in the alienation of some users, and consequently the Document of Record may become counter-productive. In addition, Alan Neville's suggestion that employers should familiarize themselves with the entire list of descriptors prior to an interview would involve a considerable amount of preparation by employers in order to use the Record of Achievement most effectively. Research which has examined employers' use of Records of Achievement in the recruitment process (Ashforth 1990; Pole 1991) indicates that they are unable to give such time to preparation. In many cases the summative Record of Achievement was used merely as a means of supporting other information such as examination results, test scores and confidential references. Moreover, research by Turner (1990) on the use of Records of Achievement in the Youth Training Scheme found that even relatively well informed intermediaries like the Careers Service and YTS Managing Agents did not use Records of Achievement systematically. Their use often depended on the individual applicant taking the initiative by bringing the document along to the interview and showing it to their interviewer.

Alan Neville's comments also highlight the issue of omission from summative documents which relates both to the length of the document and to the use of only positive statements. For example, RANSC (1989) emphasize the need for the summative record to contain only positive statements; it does not, however, address the possibility of producing an essentially negative summative record due to the omission of positive statements.

Furthermore, it has been argued (Spooner 1983) that there is no way in which success can be highlighted in a Record of Achievement which does not pinpoint failure. The fact that certain statements are made on one Record, for example, relating to punctuality or honesty, but not on another, may lead users of the Record to assume that the omission implies that the pupil is not punctual or honest. Furthermore, an evaluation of the Suffolk Record of Achievement (Bridges 1989) suggests that employers 'read between the lines', as they are used to doing with references, even when teachers had no intention that they should. In this sense, the employers were over-interpreting omissions and understatements in ways the teachers did not intend.

Phil Skelton identified this as an issue of concern, but was unable to suggest any kind of solution to the dilemmas highlighted. He stated:

> Well, you are sort of damning by omission aren't you, I understand the rationale behind it but, you know, the only way people are going to discern things is if punctuality is missing, if health is missing, you know and that takes some doing. If an employer has got a stack of those to work through, he isn't going to go through saying what's out, what's in, what's out.

The question of what kind of information should most usefully be included in a Record of Achievement was taken up by the CBI. After their general endorsement of the concept of the student profile (CBI 1980) they went on to state that it had the potential to act as a valuable aid in the recruitment of young people. They emphasized (CBI 1983) that the Record of Achievement should be presented in terms which are meaningful to employers and should address the kinds of issues which will assist their selection procedures. They identified five main areas which a national base Record of Achievement for pupils at sixteen should include. These are as follows:

1 Information about the student: e.g. date of birth, subject followed, interests, activities, etc.
2 Brief information about the school: e.g. size, location, core curriculum followed, options/examinations policy.
3 Attainment in core skills/basic abilities.
4 Examination results or other qualifications gained.
5 Personal comments/record: e.g. attendance, punctuality, dependability.

Whilst such content may be deemed to place undue emphasis on examination results and specific skills held by the individual, the CBI statement is important in outlining the kind of information which employers are likely to find useful, and in giving the support of a major employers' organization to the concept of Records of Achievement. In relation to Benton School, the final Document of Record could be seen to address all five areas specified by the CBI.

That employers value Records of Achievement in general and student summary statements in particular, can be seen from the report on the London Record of Achievement (ILEA 1988). Employers having involvement with the London Record of Achievement expressed generally positive views of summary statements. They saw them as useful for recruitment purposes and identified the following four areas on which they would wish to see pupils comment:

- Extra-curricular activities.
- What the student has experienced and been involved in.
- Plans and ambitions.
- Key achievements: how the student has developed in the last five years.

(ILEA 1988: 57)

The London employers found the student statement especially useful in providing a history about which to talk to interviewees. They also welcomed an opportunity to see samples of work which accompanied the Record of Achievement. The evidence suggests (ILEA 1988; PRAISE 1988) that information in the summative Document of Record may most profitably be seen in terms of an aid to an interview, providing a starting point for discussion (Burchell 1987). As such, Records of Achievement may not act as a basis for matching individual pupils to particular positions, but can facilitate a discussion of pupil qualities in relation to the demands and requirements of a specific job or more generally a career path.

Pupils as users

As part of this research, fifth-year pupils were questioned about the uses to which their final summative document could be put. All pupils were aware that they had a potential for use in the process of finding jobs. They spoke in terms of the summative document presenting a complete picture of themselves to the employer, which would not be available through traditional school references, reports or examination grades. Generally they were positive about the uses to which they could be put and the benefits which could be derived from their use. For example, Jason, a fifth-year pupil who was about to begin applying for jobs at the time of our discussion, made the following comment:

> I think it's probably one of its main uses [at interviews] 'cause they [employers] can see what sort of a person you are . . . they'll be able to see things they might be able to help you with and see if you've changed.

Interestingly, not only did Jason expect the summative document to prove useful in securing a job, but he also expected it to be helpful after he had started the job. By looking at the documents he believed the employer would be able to assist and target his development once in post. In Jason's opinion, therefore, the Record of Achievement was likely to maintain a relevance beyond the school and into the workplace.

Whilst Jason was the only pupil to express this particular aspiration for his Record of Achievement many fifth years had positive expectations of the contribution they could make to interview situations in particular. Debbie, a fifth year who intended to follow a career in nursing, saw their likely contribution to the interview situation in the following terms:

> There is a point [to the summative document] if there's someone who's really shy and finds it hard to talk and they go to the interview, they've got that as a back-up.

Debbie's comment is interesting in that it identifies the Record of Achievement as something to fall back on if needed. Like many of her peers she did not attribute the Record with central importance to the recruitment interview, this rested with the characteristics of the individual. In this respect, the Record was an aid to conversation which would allow the interviewer to get to know the person.

Although this expectation was held by many, not all Benton pupils had such a clear idea of the use to which their summative document might be put, and furthermore, when it should be used. Summative Documents of Record were issued to fifth-year pupils during the Spring term. This enabled pupils to make use of them for interviews with employers and colleges of further education which often took place well in advance of the end of the fifth year.

Pupils who required a completed Record of Achievement before the planned date of issue for an application or interview could be accommodated and provided with the appropriate summative documents for that purpose. However, several pupils were unsure of how the summative document related to confidential references which might be sent by the school to an employer. Others were unclear as to who was responsible for ensuring employers had access to the Record of Achievement. More than one pupil assumed it was their personal responsibility to ensure that employers received copies of the summative document, whilst others believed it was the responsibility of the school. Some were aware that employers could have access to the document only with their permission, but others assumed that they had no control over who had access, and that the document would be sent out to interested parties whether they wished it to or not. An extract from my conversation with Julie, a fifth year who was about to go for an interview for a place in an FE college, highlighted some of the confusion which existed amongst pupils.

CP: What are you going to do at the end of your fifth year Julie?

Julie: Nursery Nursing.

CP: Where at?

Julie: Midshire College.

CP: And have you got a place?

Julie: Not yet, no. I've got an interview.

CP: You've got an interview. So when you go for your interview will you take your Record of Achievement with you?

Julie: Yes.

CP: What will you do with it?

Julie: Give it to the interviewer.

CP: Actually in the interview?

Julie: Yes. But there is already one that has been sent to them isn't there?

Although in this case Julie may have been influenced by my asking if she would take the Record of Achievement with her to an interview, she was not sure of the procedure and she didn't know for certain if college personnel would have already seen her Record.

In general, those pupils who intended to continue in full-time education beyond their fifth year seemed the least sure about when to use their Record of Achievement, or if they would use it at all. For example, Johnathan, a pupil who intended to transfer to the sixth form at a Warwickshire Grammar School in order to take 'A' levels after his fifth year, was confused about the use of the Record of Achievement in the application and interview procedure. He explained:

> I think I'm going to go to a sixth form. I don't know whether you actually take them to an interview there, because it's teachers.

Johnathan believed that as he wished to transfer from one school to another within the same LEA, reports and references would exchange between the two institutions automatically. This would make the Record of Achievement largely superfluous.

Much of the confusion over the use of the summative document was highlighted in a statement made by Nicola during a group discussion held with fifth-year pupils. She remarked:

> You don't need the Record of Achievement for college, you just need your exams and you don't need it for YTS. When you've finished that you might need it then to go for a job but sometimes you might need a reference and you could come back to school, but you might be something like 21. I don't know if you can come back then and pick it up because you would be left five years.

Nicola's confusion gives rise to a range of questions relating to the use of Records of Achievement, the relationship between a traditional reference and the possession of a Record of Achievement, the time-span over which pupils can expect to have access to their Records. More specifically, Nicola was unclear as to whether the Record of Achievement was relevant only to those seeking employment as opposed to further education or YTS, whether the possession of a Record of Achievement precluded the pupil from seeking a traditional reference from school and whether it would be possible to collect her Record several years after leaving.

Clearly, Nicola was confused about a number of fundamental issues relating to the summative Record of Achievement and although confusion to this extent was not common amongst the fifth years interviewed, many did share at least one of these misunderstandings with her.

Several pupils who had experience of using their Record of Achievement in a job interview found that it made a positive contribution to dialogue with the interviewer. For example, Sarah and Kathy recalled their experiences with employers. Kathy explained:

CP: . . . so did they [the interviewers] refer to your Record of Achievement while you were there [At the interview]?

Kathy: Yes.

CP: What sort of things did they say?

Kathy: They said it was a really good idea really, it showed them what sort of a person I was, because they don't just want a person who can cook or clean or whatever. They've got to have the right sort of personality to get through the long hours and, they said it was a good idea.

CP: And the Record of Achievement was able to show all that?

Kathy: Yes, they also said that it's good that your school still has prefects and things and puts it on there [the Record of Achievement] because it shows that you are a responsible person.

Kathy had experienced a positive reaction from her interviewer, not only to her own profile, but also to the general concept of the Record of Achievement. It enabled her to approach the interview from a position of strength. The interviewer had an account of her accomplishments and qualities which he was able to draw on as a basis for the conversation. As Kathy explained, the ensuing conversation enabled aspects of her personality to be revealed which she considered to be important for the job. In Sarah's case the apparent unfamiliarity of her interviewers with Records of Achievement necessitated that she explain to them the process by which they were produced. She recalled:

CP: Did you talk about yours [Record of Achievement] when you were in your interview then Sarah?

Sarah: Yes.

CP: What sort of things did you say?

Sarah: . . . they didn't quite understand how it worked, and they were asking me how to decide which one of those [the descriptors] fitted me. And I had to explain.

CP: So you had to talk about the process of it, a little like we're talking now. And were they impressed with it?

Sarah: Yes they were, very.

Again, in Sarah's experience the Record of Achievement acted as a talking point in the interview. Moreover, it also highlights the important question of the extent to which employers and other end-users are familiar with and know how to use Records of Achievement.

ILEA (1988), Ashforth (1990) and Pole (1991) detail generally favourable responses from employers towards the concept of Records of Achievement and to summative documents, but their work also shows that recruiters know little of the way in which they are used, or of their objectives. If the experience of Sarah proves to be common amongst pupils presenting Records to employers, it would seem that an important means of employers learning about Records of Achievement is from pupils themselves. Moreover, if Records of Achievement are to be issued to all school-leavers (RANSC 1989; DES 1991) in the future, it emphasizes the need for a comprehensive programme to raise end-users' awareness of them. In particular to educate employers in their use. Action to achieve these aims will be required both at national and local levels.

The experiences of Sarah and Kathy seem to have been very positive. In spite of this, however, neither of the girls thought their Record of Achievement had helped them to any great extent in securing the positions for which they had been interviewed. Both felt their own personal disposition, together with the qualifications which they held or expected to hold had made the biggest impression on the interviewer. From my conversation with the two girls it became clear that they viewed the Record of Achievement as one of a number of things which they would employ to facilitate a successful interview. For Kathy and Sarah and several other fifth years Records of Achievement served a similar purpose to a curriculum vitae, to personal references and to examination results. Ultimately it was a combination of these factors, together with the way in which the individual presented himself or herself at the interview which determined whether or not he or she got the job. In this respect, the Record of Achievement formed part of a package of things which the pupil could utilize. For example, Craig, a fifth year who was in the process of applying for jobs, explained how he expected to use his Record of Achievement to assist him, both in getting an interview, and with the interview itself. He stated:

I've applied for quite a few jobs now to engineering firms and sent off a letter of application and a curriculum vitae and my Record of Achievement, but when it comes round to them interviewing me I think you'd normally give them your Record of Achievement to look over, with your references.

In this case the Record of Achievement was just one of the tools which the pupil could use in applying for jobs. Craig did not see the Record of Achievement as something which could be used on its own. He had chosen to use it in combination with other more traditional instruments which would also provide detailed information to a prospective employer.

In Benton School, however, the head and several teachers placed great emphasis on the Record of Achievement in the recruitment process. For example, the head had informed many local employers that he would prefer not to produce confidential references on pupils, as he believed the Summative Document of Record which contained information on academic achievement, out-of-school activities and the agreed statement written jointly by teacher and pupil, would provide all the information they required. Several teachers expressed serious concern over this decision and anticipated that employers would see it in terms of the school refusing to co-operate with them. As such, they saw the decision as detrimental to the interests of the pupils. In addition, the actions of Craig and other pupils who regarded the Record of Achievement as only one of the tools which they could use to help find a job, implies that they too questioned the expectation that Records of Achievement would provide all the information required by employers. Evidence from studies of their use by employers (Ashforth 1990; Pole 1991) suggests that they were right to do so.

Ownership

The intention to send out copies of the summative Document of Record to employers and other users raises the issue of ownership of the information contained therein. The RANSC Report (1989) states that ownership of the Record of Achievement and hence decisions of the use to which it might be put and of who should have access to it, rest with the pupil. Before heads and/or teachers despatch copies of the Record to prospective employers it is, therefore, incumbent upon them to obtain the permission of the pupil in order to do so. At Benton School, pupils were informed of their rights to restrict access to the Record of Achievement and were asked to give written permission to allow the head to use it as he saw appropriate. Technically, therefore, the pupil, had control of the document. In practice, very few refused permission for the head to use it as he saw fit. Whilst none of the pupils alluded to being coerced or persuaded into giving such permission, the decision to do so must be seen in the context of teacher–pupil or rather pupil–headteacher relationships. In this situation the relative status of the two parties, together with the fact that David Fox had made clear his desire to use the summative Records in place of traditional references, surely acted to place pressure on the pupil to grant the permission. Refusal to do so may have resulted in bad feeling between the two parties and furthermore, with such emphasis being placed on the Record of Achievement, the pupil could not be sure of the kind or format of alternative information which would be made available to employers and other users. Giving permission was, probably the easiest path for the pupil to take even if he or she had reservations about it.

The way in which schools give pupils ownership of their Records clearly requires careful attention. In the case of Benton School pupils were given ownership and the right to control access to them, but the way in which this was done seemed to make anything but agreement by the pupil very difficult. By giving general permission for the head to use the documents as he saw fit, the pupil had effectively lost control of them. Whilst this is not to suggest that the head would use the documents in any way which was detrimental to the pupils, the Benton case serves to illustrate that the issue of ownership may not always be straightforward. Ownership is an important issue for Records of Achievement. Failure to give pupils ownership and effective control of their Records of Achievement is to contravene not only the guidelines which have been devised over recent years (DES 1984; RANSC 1989), but also the ethic upon which the process is based. Pupil ownership of the Record must be seen as part of the move towards pupils taking greater control of the learning situation.

A range of issues have been highlighted in this chapter which require careful consideration in relation to the development of summative Documents of Record and for promoting their use by employers, college admissions' tutors, parents and pupils. Unlike pupils encountered by Swales (1979) there was a general feeling amongst Benton pupils that the summative document was worth while and could be useful in their transfer from school to work (cf. Brennan 1988). There appeared to be some confusion amongst pupils, however, relating to the process of actually using the document. In particular, pupils were confused as to whether it was their responsibility or the schools to ensure that employers received a copy of their Record of Achievement. The question of timing was also raised (cf. PRAISE 1988); for example, should documents be sent prior to interviews, with an application form or presented during an interview? Furthermore, some pupils claimed not to have considered using their summative document for job-seeking purposes and two pupils claimed not to know that a summative document existed.

In particular, confusion existed over the relevance of the Document of Record amongst those pupils who intended to continue in full-time education after the end of their fifth year. Several were unconvinced of the suitability of the document for application to FE colleges and sixth forms. They expected more attention to be given to examination results and confidential references from the school.

In most cases where confusion existed it would seem to be based either on pupils' lack of knowledge, or simply on them having forgotten about the summative document. Whilst pupils may be seen to derive most value from the processes involved with recording achievement (Burgess and Adams 1986; Munby 1989) it is also important to recognize and capitalize on the summative aspects of the process (Brennan 1988; Andrews 1988). For some pupils and some teachers the summative document and its potential to assist in the job market may be perceived as the principal role of Records of Achievement (cf. Stronach 1989).

The experiences of staff and pupils in Benton School have emphasized the need to ensure that all pupils are aware of the ways in which their summative documents may be used prior to beginning the search for work or a place in further education. For example, Ashley, a fifth-year pupil seeking a place in further education, explained why he did not use his Record of Achievement at an interview at an FE college. His case illustrated the need for pupils to be constantly reminded about the purpose of the summative document. Our conversation was as follows:

> CP: And will you use your Record of Achievement in your interview?
> *Ashley*: I don't know.
> CP: Don't know, why not?
> *Ashley*: Well I haven't used it for the first interview because I didn't think about it.
> CP: You didn't think about it?
> *Ashley*: No because it was a long time ago since we did Records of Achievement. The end of last year because I'm first in the register.

Ashley simply forgot about using his Record of Achievement because it had been a long time since his negotiation session. His case shows the need to talk to pupils about their possible use during tutorial time, PSE lessons or careers sessions. By doing this, Records of Achievement will surely cease to be seen as 'events' which occur at a particular time of year.

The success of the summative Record of Achievement may, to a great extent, rest with the degree to which they are able to meet the objectives and expectations of the DES (1984) and RANSC (1989) who sought to promote their development and use, and also live up to the claims of Broadfoot (1982) Garforth and Macintosh (1986) and Stansbury (1985) amongst others who assert that Records of Achievement have the capacity to provide the kind of detail for employers which was not previously possible just with examination results and school reports. In this respect Stronach (1989) sees Records of Achievement as a marketing tool for schools which acts primarily to the benefit of employers by removing some of the risks associated with recruitment of young people. Whilst Stronach makes a number of important ethical points about the development of Records of Achievement, if their use in recruitment procedures results in a better fit between pupils and jobs, then this must surely be advantageous for both the school-leaver and the employer.

In order for Records of Achievement to prove useful employers (who through previous experience have been shown to be slow to embrace and understand new initiatives in education (cf. Eggleston 1984; Sims 1987)), parents and ultimately to pupils there is a need for them to be used effectively. This case study of Benton School has highlighted the need for user education in terms of Records of Achievement. Such education needs to go beyond basic awareness raising to include an understanding of the process and rationale for Records of Achievement.

Parents of Benton pupils, together with local employers were positively disposed towards this new form of reporting and recording and there existed an opportunity to capitalize upon their reactions by ensuring that it was fully understood. In several cases Benton pupils acted as ambassadors for Records of Achievement informing their parents and employers of their purpose and content and about the process by which they were produced. However, not all pupils were able to fulfil such a role. The case study has exposed a substantial minority of pupils who were themselves unclear about the purpose of the Record of Achievement and in particular under what circumstances they could use it. It seems likely that pupils will remain the best ambassadors for Records of Achievement and a principal means by which they are brought to the attention of parents, employers and other potential users. By increasing awareness in this way, pupils should themselves be the ultimate beneficiaries. For all concerned, however, this process seems likely to be most effective if it is embarked upon from a position of knowledge and understanding.

7

CONCLUSION

An overview

This study of Benton School has presented a picture of a Record of Achievement process which has been established in the school for several years. It has attempted to show the Record of Achievement not in isolation but in a wider school and social context. It has, therefore, highlighted issues which were central to the day-to-day management of the school and to the experiences of staff and pupils.

The analysis of the Record of Achievement process has taken as its focus the views and experiences of the staff and the pupils. These views and experiences have been represented by the actual conversation of teachers and pupils recorded during the interviews which I conducted with them. A picture of the Record of Achievement process has been drawn largely from these conversations and from observations in the school.

In collecting and analysing these primary data it has been my intention to represent the feelings and experiences of the staff and pupils, by highlighting particular areas of concern which they raised during the course of the research. The issues which the case study addresses, therefore, are, in this sense the concerns of the teachers and the pupils. My role as researcher has been largely to interpret, analyse and articulate these concerns.

The case study has identified and explored a wide range of issues which have been central to the development of Records of Achievement. These issues will surely resonate with teachers and administrators who are attempting to introduce or develop similar methods of reporting and recording in schools throughout the United Kingdom. In particular, attention has been given to the school, its size, both in terms of pupil population and the number of staff, and to its location in respect to the significance of the rural location and its relevance to the out-of-school activities of the pupils. The case study has also considered the history of Records of Achievement in Benton School and its progress from a limited pilot activity to an important whole-school approach to recording and assessment. As part of this, the role of the head and deputy and other staff responsible for the promotion and development of the Record of Achievement has also been discussed.

In this context, the experiences of Benton School have shown that the integration of Records of Achievement with recording and reporting procedures is a developmental process. The Benton Record of Achievement has undergone a number of changes as the process has matured. For example, changes to lists of descriptors have been introduced, computer software now plays a bigger part in the process, the timing of negotiation sessions has changed and the format of the document of record has changed several times. It would seem that change is endemic to Records of Achievement. If they are an integral part of teaching and learning in any school then this is surely desirable. Records of Achievement are process based, they are about reviewing and looking towards future development. In this respect they need to change as the school changes, and as part of the review process they need to review their own contribution to reporting and recording and the experience of teaching and learning.

The research has also looked at the role of Records of Achievement as change agents in Benton School. Whilst there is evidence to suggest that the process had contributed to change in such areas as teacher–pupil relations, pupil motivation and teaching styles, it would be incorrect to attribute Records of Achievement as the principal agents of change in these areas. Staff suggested that although Records of Achievement were an important innovation in the school the affect on teaching style, pastoral care, school organization, pupil motivation, etc. could not always be distinguished from other concurrent changes in education (Hargreaves *et al.* 1988). For example, TVEI was seen as a particularly important innovation (cf. Stoney *et al.* 1986; Gleeson 1987; Hinckley *et al.* 1987; Dale *et al.* 1990) which necessitated change in many areas. Similarly, GCSE brought changes (cf. Scott 1989) not only to assessment but also to teaching style and coursework commitment. More recently the impact of the National Curriculum (Simon 1988; Moon 1990) has brought wide-scale change to the school. Amidst this general milieu of educational innovation it proved difficult for teachers to attribute particular change to any single initiative or development. Where changes had occurred they were seen to be a result of a combination of factors.

Negotiation

In terms of the process and procedures which have been established for the Record of Achievement, particular attention has been given the role of negotiation, its definition and centrality to the process and to goal setting. Discussion has been concerned with the contribution of both negotiation and goal setting to the individual development of the pupil. Associated with issues of negotiation and goal setting has been the question of the extent to which Records of Achievement pose a challenge to the authority and the traditional position of the teacher. Questions of pupils accepting responsibility for their own learning programmes have been discussed.

The issue of time has also been central to this case study, especially in relation to the amount of time required to conduct effective teacher–pupil negotiations and the time commitment from teachers for the completion of large numbers of descriptor sheets.

Cross-curricular recording

Important issues have been raised within this study about cross-curricular recording procedures which the Benton Record of Achievement necessitated. For example all subject teachers were required to appraise pupils according to the same set of descriptors. Some difficulties with this approach have been highlighted where individual subject teachers expressed concern that the range of descriptors did not adequately describe the skills and qualities inherent in their subjects. It would seem pertinent to ask, therefore, whether the list of descriptors was always commensurate with the objectives of the individual subjects? For example, Alan Neville, an English teacher, felt there was nothing in the descriptor bank which focused on pupils' ability to understand and work with English literature texts. At the same time he regarded as absurd the fact that he could, if he so wished, comment on their ability in relation to mental calculations (descriptor 15), measuring (descriptor 17) and micro-computer skills (descriptor 19) when they had little or no relevance to his subject area. Similarly, George James, a Science teacher expressed the view that the descriptors were too general and failed to address pupils' ability to handle scientific concepts.

The reliance on wide ranging descriptor banks required teachers to comment on an amalgamation of subject specific, cross-curricular skills and personal qualities. For teachers to make judgements against these three different kinds of skills and qualities was demanding, and assumed that similar cognitive and developmental processes underpinned skills and qualities and furthermore, that they could be judged by the same criteria. Given that it was unlikely that all staff would be able to develop the same level of knowledge of all pupils, the criteria and evidence upon which staff based their comments and judgements was, as one teacher admitted, in some cases, spurious.

Power and control

The data have also highlighted a series of important issues which relate to power and control. The official rhetoric of Records of Achievement is that they foster a more equal relationship between teachers and pupils (DES 1984; RANSC 1989). The outward signs in Benton School suggested that attempts had been made to facilitate a closer relationship between the two parties. For example, the emphasis, which was placed on negotiation, the negotiation room and the interest shown by teachers in pupils' out-of-school activities appeared to have created an impression of enhanced status for the pupils in the school. It has been shown, however, that this impression was not always carried through into practice. For example, pupils described negotiation sessions when little discussion or exchange between the teacher and pupil took place. Moreover, some pupils described a situation of confrontation where teachers were concerned primarily to persuade pupils to accept their own and their colleagues' interpretation of the situation. In such situations, the pupil was undoubtedly in a subordinate position from which it was difficult to engage in effective discussion with his or her tutor. Furthermore, one member of staff admitted to using the Record of Achievement as a threat to pupils, in an effort to achieve better discipline in the classroom. She explained:

> Sometimes when they won't put all the equipment away at the end of the lesson, I tell them that I shall be filling in their Records of Achievement later.

In this instance the Record of Achievement was not used to enhance teacher–pupil relations or to equalize any status differentials. Much like the traditional school report it was used to emphasize the position of the teacher standing in judgement over the pupils. In this case the Record of Achievement had been used specifically as a tool of control. Although the occasions when it was used in such a way were probably rare, the example serves to illustrate the point that Records of Achievement do have the potential to subordinate the pupil as well as to create relationships of greater equality. To assume, however, that with the introduction of a Record of Achievement, teachers and pupils will become equal partners in a learning environment is surely to ignore a whole range of issues relating the socialization of school pupils, the social class, race and gender of teachers and pupils and the organization of schools and schooling. The interaction of these important variables which produce success and failure, subordinate and superordinate, teachers and pupils, ultimately, seems to outweigh many of the effects of a new recording and reporting system.

Summative records

Finally, attention has also been given to the format and use of the Document of Record. The responses of parents to the summative documents have been examined as have pupils' intentions with regard to their use. Above all the study has emphasized the need for effective education in the use of summative documents, not just for pupils but also for employers, admissions tutors of colleges, polytechnics and universities, and also for teachers in schools where the record is developed. Summative Records of Achievement will only be successful if they become a common and accepted part of recruitment procedures. For this to happen schools have a responsibility to publicize their records on a local scale. The DES and the careers service, meanwhile, have the means to raise the status of Records of Achievement nationally.

Rhetoric and reality

In general, the research has shown that Records of Achievement received high priority in Benton School. The head and the majority of staff were committed to them. Similarly, pupils in the main, accepted the Record of Achievement process as part of normal school procedures. The amount of time given to Records of Achievement, the physical manifestations of it (the negotiation room, the notice-board and lockers in the staffroom), together with the emphasis placed on it as the principal means of recording and reporting pupil progress and development, suggested a high level of integration with the fundamental aims of and approach to teaching and learning in Benton School.

However, the data have revealed a gap between the rhetoric of what the Head and several other staff would like to believe was happening and the school implementation of the Record of Achievement process. For example, whilst the head constantly spoke of a reporting and recording system which was integrated with the curriculum and had major implications for the way in which teachers approached their jobs, evidence from staff and pupils suggested that this was not the case. For example, pupils tended to speak of Records of Achievement as an event which occurred at a particular time of year rather than an ongoing process, as my conversation with Luke, a fourth-year pupil, underlined:

CP: What are Record of Achievements about then Luke?
Luke: We have the forms and you have to say what you think
        of yourself.

CP: What you think of yourself?

Luke: And work, yes, how well you cope with the work. Different things you have to tick off.

CP: So that's what it's all about then?

Luke: It's about writing down your achievements, in and out of school.

Like most pupils who were faced with the general question, 'what are Records of Achievement about?' Luke referred to specific components of the process. Whilst his answer was not incorrect it illustrated that pupils tended to see Records of Achievement as a series of discrete events rather than as an holistic process. Pupils usually answered the question with reference to the negotiation sessions or the documentation which they were required to complete. Their answers suggested that Records of Achievement were seen to happen at particular times of the year and in this sense they were not ongoing.

Comments from the staff revealed a similar view. For example, several spoke in terms of 'getting through' their Records of Achievement or referred to specific non-teaching periods as Record of Achievement time. They too were identifying Records of Achievements as a series of tasks to be conducted rather than an ongoing process. In addition, their concern about the time required to carry out the various tasks suggested that many Benton teachers saw the Record of Achievement as a set of extra or additional duties which they were required to perform. They were not generally seen as integral to the curriculum or to teaching and learning processes.

Whilst it is difficult to attribute staff views and approaches to Records of Achievement to a single reason, the Benton process tended to emphasize one particular component above all others. That of negotiation. To facilitate the negotiation great importance was placed on the collection of information via descriptor sheets completed by all relevant teachers. Furthermore, the final two years of the process saw the introduction of the computer to the negotiation sessions which brought with it a whole set of concerns about teacher competence and confidence with software and hardware (cf. Skinsley 1986; Pole 1991). The effect of this emphasis on negotiation was that a complex bureaucracy was built up around the process. As a result staff and pupils became increasingly concerned with conducting the individual components of the Record of

Achievement and in so doing tended to lose sight of the overall aim of the process. In this sense, the concern to establish an effective machinery seemed to establish the Record of Achievement as a series of additional tasks. As a result the process may have militated against the aim to become an integral part of teaching and learning.

The case study has brought to light, therefore, an absence of fit between the rhetoric and promise of Records of Achievement espoused by the head within the school and by national 'promoters' (e.g. DES 1984; RANSC 1989) and the practice and experience of teachers and pupils in several important areas. Above all, it has highlighted the complexities inherent in the process. It has also raised questions about issues which are central to the purpose of the school, to processes of teaching and learning and to education *per se*. For example, discussion has focused on teacher–pupil relations, teaching styles, control and discipline, pupil motivation, reporting and recording, assessment and the role of the school *vis-à-vis* employers and the transfer from school to work.

The range of issues highlighted has shown that Records of Achievement may be much more than a new means of recording and reporting pupil progress. They may have the potential to operate as change agents in schools and to help teachers consider some fundamental questions about what they wish to achieve and how they might achieve it. The case study has focused on a school which has sought to integrate the Record of Achievement process with its everyday approach to teaching and learning. It has taken a whole-school approach which has sought to place the Record of Achievement at the centre of its activities. Much of what it has done could only be achieved with the commitment of many of its staff and parents and the co-operation of the pupils.

However, much of the work in the introduction and development of Records of Achievement in Benton and many other schools may now be threatened. The government failed to make Records of Achievement mandatory and the national Record of Achievement currently being promoted by the DES leaves their use to the discretion of individual heads and teachers. Furthermore, testing arrangements for all pupils in maintained schools, introduced as a result of the 1988 Educational Reform Act, now make it unlikely that schools will be able to use Records of Achievement as their principal means of recording and reporting on pupil progress. The pressure to publish test results in order to attract more pupils to the school and hence, under LMS, to increase funds (Simon 1988) may mean that schools are forced away from holistic reporting to crude methods which facilitate simplistic comparisons between schools. If this proves to be the case, then the capacity of Records of Achievement to provide contextual and meaningful information about pupils and schools will have been sadly overlooked.

Nevertheless the experiences at Benton School have demonstrated the capacity of Records of Achievement to communicate between schools and parents, schools and industry and teachers and pupils. It would be possible for Records of Achievement to incorporate results of national tests in such a way as to make them meaningful in terms of important social and educational factors which may be particular to the school or the individual pupil. In this respect, Records of Achievement may bring to the attention of the wider public the kinds of things that go on in individual schools and demonstrate the successes of pupils attending those schools. The supply and demand model to which schools seem likely to be forced to work under LMS (Simon 1988) may place increased significance on the Record of Achievement as a form of 'advertising' to industry and to parents. In a crude instrumental way the rationale for the Record of Achievement may be seen in terms of its capacity to demonstrate to employers and parents, the positive qualities of the school and the benefits to be derived from enrolling their children at that school or recruiting new workers from it. In this context the Record of Achievement is a means of bringing to the attention of the wider world the achievements of the pupils and hence of the school. If successful, the school can look forward to an enhanced reputation, to more pupils and consequently more income. Far from being inappropriate for reporting on pupil progress and achievements in the national curriculum, the Record of Achievement has the potential to provide information on pupil and school performance which is meaningful and goes far beyond crude league table comparisons. The Record of Achievement can provide an opportunity for schools to demonstrate to interested parties the scope of their activities and the real achievements of their pupils.

Reviewing the process

The case study has highlighted many areas to which Benton and other schools could usefully give some thought. The fact that the school had some five years experience of Records of Achievement meant that a certain degree of experimentation with the process had taken place and moderation and refinements had ensued. However, the fact that Records of Achievement were seen by the head and many of the staff to be integral to the functions of the school implied that they could not remain static, but must change and develop as the school changed and developed. The fact that Records of Achievement involved not merely an end-product but a process, implied that change and development was integral to them.

To facilitate effective change and development schools will need to continually review their Record of Achievement process. In this respect the following questions are posed as an aid to such a review.

1 To what extent are the aims and objectives of the Record of Achievement process understood and accepted by all staff and by pupils and parents?
2 To what extent are staff and pupils able to influence the process?
3 How much emphasis is placed on the role and perspective of the pupil in the process?
4 To what extent is the process driven by the use of predetermined descriptors?
5 How far can cross-curricular descriptors take account of subject-specific qualities?
6 Is the language of the descriptors understood by all pupils and staff?
7 How much negotiation actually takes place in the pupil–teacher discussion sessions?
8 Is negotiation the correct term to use, or does it imply confrontation and the need for exchange?
9 Is a specific negotiation room always the best place for teacher–pupil discussions?
10 Are any gender and/or racial differences apparent in the process?
11 To what extent is the process used as a means of exercising control, either overtly or covertly, over pupils?
12 To what extent is goal setting regarded as important by pupils and staff?
13 To what extent does goal setting contribute to the development of the pupil?

14 Are pupils fully aware of the potential uses of the Document of
    Record and of their ownership of it?

The questions are drawn from the issues arising from the case study;
the list is not exhaustive, but is offered as an aid to reflection and
consideration of the way in which the Record of Achievement process may be developed. As such, the questions are not posed in a
negative sense but as a means of self-evaluation through which the
process may be enhanced.

DESCRIPTOR SHEETS

For use with:

A: 2nd and 3rd Years

B: 4th and 5th Years

A

NAME _____ FORM _____ STAFF CODE _____

1.0 Self

1.1 ☐ I always enjoy school.
     ☐ I think school's all right.
     ☐ I don't like school much.

1.2 ☐ I always take pride in how I look.
     ☐ I am nearly always clean and tidy.
     ☐ I am not bothered how I look.

1.3 ☐ I make sure I bring the right books and equipment.
     ☐ I mostly bring them.
     ☐ I often forget to bring them.
     ☐ I don't care whether I have them or not.

1.4   ☐   I always try my best, even if the teacher leaves me to work on my own.
      ☐   I need the teacher from time to time to encourage me.
      ☐   I only work when the teacher makes me.

1.5   When I do tests or exams:
      ☐   I produce my very best work.
      ☐   I do about the same as in lesson time.
      ☐   I don't do as well as in lesson time.
      ☐   I'm likely to go to pieces.

1.6   When I have to make my mind up about something:
      ☐   I consider it from all points of view.
      ☐   I think about it for a bit.
      ☐   I do the first thing that comes into my head.

1.7   If a teacher criticizes my work:
      ☐   I try to do better next time.
      ☐   I am not put off.
      ☐   I am too fed up to bother again.

1.8   If something embarrassing happens to me:
      ☐   I don't show how I feel.
      ☐   I usually get over it quickly.
      ☐   I get upset or cannot control my feelings.

1.9   ☐   I like to tackle something new.
      ☐   I like doing things I am used to.

1.10   If I cannot get my own way:
      ☐   I just keep on about it.
      ☐   I make the best of it.
      ☐   I have a moan.
      ☐   I sulk quietly.
      ☐   I cry.
      ☐   I go away.
      ☐   I get angry.
      ☐   I hit out.

1.11   If someone really upsets me:
      ☐   I forget about it quickly.
      ☐   I feel upset for a while.
      ☐   I keep on until I get my own back.

1.12   I often suddenly feel miserable for no reason:
      ☐   Yes   ☐   No

1.13   Which of these fits you best:
      ☐   I prefer to keep a friend for a long time.
      ☐   I prefer to keep changing my friends.

2.0 Relationships with others

2.1   Which do you usually like best?:
- [ ] Being with lots of people of your own age.
- [ ] Being with several people of your own age.
- [ ] Being with one friend.
- [ ] Being on your own.
- [ ] Being with adults.

2.2   In the group:
- [ ] You are the one who is always at the centre of things.
- [ ] You join in willingly.

2.3
- [ ] You always seem to know how everybody is feeling.
- [ ] You only really tune in with the feelings of your friends.
- [ ] You don't seem to bother how other people feel.

2.4   Talking to adults in school:
- [ ] You find it easy to hold a conversation with anyone you meet.
- [ ] You talk best with adults you know.
- [ ] You find it difficult to hold a conversation.

2.5*   You seem to know how to behave with the following people:

	Yes	No
School staff	[ ]	[ ]
Visitors to school	[ ]	[ ]

2.6
- [ ] You stick to the school rules.
- [ ] You sometimes don't observe the school rules.
- [ ] You often break school rules.

3.0 School work

3.1
- [ ] You seem alert and keen to do your best in most lessons.
- [ ] Your interest and attention varies from one lesson to another.
- [ ] You find it difficult to concentrate because you've other things on your mind.
- [ ] You find it hard to keep your mind on work and you don't bother to try.

3.2
- [ ] You pick the right things to do most jobs.
- [ ] You generally need to be told what things to use.

3.3
- [ ] You can carry out quite difficult instructions spoken by the teacher.
- [ ] You usually understand what the teacher tells you.
- [ ] You have a job to follow what the teacher is saying.

3.4
- [ ] You can easily explain anything to anybody.
- [ ] You can explain most things to people.
- [ ] You find it hard to say what you mean.

3.5 ☐ You can easily look anything up in reference books in the classroom and the library.

☐ You can find out what you want to know from books the teacher provides.

☐ You have a bit of a struggle with many books.

3.6 ☐ You can use the information you have gathered to present your point of view in writing.

☐ You can write answers to questions about a passage you have read.

☐ You find most written work difficult.

3.7 Your work generally is:

☐ Tidy and attractively laid out.

☐ Clear and easily followed.

☐ Untidy and disorganized.

☐ Scruffy and messy.

3.8 You seem to do your best work:

☐ In a group.

☐ With one other person.

☐ On your own.

3.9 You prefer to do your own work:

☐ In the classroom.

☐ In the library.

☐ At home.

☐ At a friend's house.

☐ In the local library.

B

Personal and social qualities

1.0 Cheerfulness
1.1 ☐ Remains cheerful in the face of difficulty.
1.2 ☐ Soon regains cheerfulness after any setback.
1.3 ☐ Except for the occasional 'low' is cheerful.
1.4 ☐ Is easily depressed when faced with problems with either schoolwork or relationships.
1.5 ☐ Rarely appears to be happy and cheerful in school.

2.0 Helpfulness
2.1 ☐ Sees where help is needed and readily gives it.
2.2 ☐ When he/she does see that help is needed he/she gives it.
2.3 ☐ When asked for help he/she gives it.

2.4 ☐ Is reluctant to give help to others.
2.5 ☐ Never volunteers to give help to others.
2.6 ☐ Avoids being helpful if possible.

3.0 Open-mindedness
3.1 ☐ Understands and respects other people's points of view.
3.2 ☐ Is prepared to reflect upon the opinions of others.
3.3 ☐ Is prepared to listen to the opinions of others.
3.4 ☐ Rarely gives proper consideration to the opinions of other people.
3.5 ☐ Is not prepared to listen to, nor to consider the opinions of other people.

4.0 Responding to an emergency
4.1 ☐ Keeps a cool head and takes the lead in an emergency.
4.2 ☐ Keeps cool and gives a helping hand in an emergency.
4.3 ☐ Carries out instructions calmly in an emergency.
4.4 ☐ Has never been involved in an emergency but believes he/she will remain calm.
4.5 ☐ Is inclined to panic easily.

5.0 Perseverance
5.1 ☐ Always tries to see a task through.
5.2 ☐ Tries to complete tasks which interest him/her.
5.3 ☐ Needs encouragement to see a task through.
5.4 ☐ Shows little determination in dealing properly with tasks.
5.5 ☐ Shows little inclination to see a task through unless closely supervised.
5.6 ☐ Unable to persevere with a task for any length of time even when given encouragement.

6.0 Punctuality
6.1 ☐ Is punctual.
6.2 ☐ Is occasionally late to school and to lessons.
6.3 ☐ Is often late.
6.4 ☐ Lateness is a very serious problem.

7.0 Reliability
7.1 ☐ Can be depended upon to carry out what he/she has undertaken to do.
7.2 ☐ Can usually be relied upon to carry out any task that he/she undertakes.
7.3 ☐ Has shown himself/herself to be unreliable on a number of occasions.

8.0 Self-assurance
8.1 ☐ Is realistically confident about the skills he/she possesses.

8.2   ☐   Is confident in familiar work situations.
8.3   ☐   With support is confident in familiar work situations.
8.4   ☐   Is confident in the company of his/her peer group.
8.5   ☐   Is reserved and diffident in the company of adults.
8.6   ☐   Shows little confidence in his/her own abilities.

9.0 Sociability
9.1   ☐   A popular and central figure with a wide circle of friends.
9.2   ☐   Forms and maintains good relationships with fellow pupils and adults.
9.3   ☐   Whilst getting on well with a small group of friends he/she finds it difficult to form relationships with other people.
9.4   ☐   Is able to mix well with fellow pupils but prefers to be alone.
9.5   ☐   Relationships with others can be spoilt by a lack of self-restraint.
9.6   ☐   Has only one or two friends.
9.7   ☐   Has great difficulty in relating to anyone outside the immediate family.

10.0 Sense of responsibility
10.1   ☐   Has a mature and responsible attitude to self and others.
10.2   ☐   Takes the responsibility for the consequences of his/her own actions.
10.3   ☐   Sometimes needs reminding of his/her own responsibilities.
10.4   ☐   Occasionally behaves in an irresponsible manner.
10.5   ☐   Often behaves in an irresponsible manner.

Work and study skills

1.0 Working with others
1.1   ☐   Recognizes the needs of the groups and is prepared to take a positive lead.
1.2   ☐   Well motivated in group activities.
1.3   ☐   Is prepared to work with others when given a task.
1.4   ☐   Prefers to work on his/her own whenever possible.
1.5   ☐   Finds it difficult to work with other people.
1.6   ☐   Can be disruptive in a working-group situation.
1.7   ☐   Is compelled to work alone so that group work can progress unhindered.

2.0 Ability to work independently
2.1   ☐   Shows outstanding capacity for organizing his/her work and time effectively.
2.2   ☐   Shows a considerable capacity for organizing his/her work and time effectively.

2.3 ☐ Always works to his/her maximum potential regardless of supervision.

2.4 ☐ A minimum of supervision is required to enable him/her to complete work.

2.5 ☐ Homework tasks are generally completed satisfactorily.

2.6 ☐ Though not regularly completed, homework tasks are of an adequate standard when produced.

2.7 ☐ Needs help and/or motivation in order to fulfil a task set although he/she can sometimes work without supervision.

2.8 ☐ Does not show much inclination to spend time in organizing his/her work effectively.

3.0 Listening
3.1 ☐ Listens and responds to ideas and detailed instructions with a high level of understanding.

3.2 ☐ Accurately recalls what is said to him/her and acts upon it.

3.3 ☐ Listens to brief instructions and carries them out accurately.

3.4 ☐ Is sometimes inattentive and misunderstands instructions.

3.5 ☐ Rarely listens carefully to what is being said and as a result his/her response is inadequate and/or inaccurate.

4.0 Oral explanation
4.1 ☐ Presents a lengthy, fluent, reasoned argument.

4.2 ☐ Clearly explains a complex process.

4.3 ☐ Explains a process clearly and accurately.

4.4 ☐ Explains what he/she is doing.

4.5 ☐ Has a very limited vocabulary and finds it difficult to explain clearly what he/she is doing.

4.6 ☐ Is very reluctant to attempt oral explanation except in very informal situations.

5.0 Talking with others
5.1 ☐ Speaks confidently and persuasively in a group.

5.2 ☐ Is an intelligent, amusing, conversationalist who expresses himself/herself interestingly on a number of different topics.

5.3 ☐ Makes effective contributions to group discussions.

5.4 ☐ Has no difficulty in expressing himself/herself in a variety of situations but does not always do so fluently.

5.5 ☐ Asks clearly what he/she needs to know.

5.6 ☐ Is reluctant to participate in classroom discussion and does not find personal conversation easy with adults.

5.7 ☐ Replies coherently if he/she is spoken to.

5.8 ☐ Finds difficulty in expressing himself/herself clearly and is particularly unresponsive in formal conversations.

6.0 Reading

6.1 ☐ Reads and understands material presented in a variety of written forms.

6.2 ☐ Follows successfully a series of written instructions and uses when necessary everyday reference sources, e.g. dictionary.

6.3 ☐ Reads and understands basic instructions, notices and messages.

6.4 ☐ Reads and understands simple written material with assistance.

6.5 ☐ Is unable to use alphabetical lists or to organize written material properly.

6.6 ☐ Finds difficulty in understanding any kind of written material even with assistance.

7.0 Writing

7.1 ☐ Writes accurately and appropriately for a wide variety of purposes.

7.2 ☐ Writes with an acceptable standard of accuracy in spelling, punctuation and grammar.

7.3 ☐ Writes clear factual explanations.

7.4 ☐ Uses a vocabulary which is adequate for everyday written work.

7.5 ☐ Writes short directions, instructions and messages.

7.6 ☐ Writes short messages.

7.7 ☐ Has a very limited vocabulary and has difficulty spelling and punctuating even simple written work.

7.8 ☐ Needs assistance to produce even the simplest written work.

8.0 Memory

8.1 ☐ Accurately recalls complicated ideas and gets them in the right order.

8.2 ☐ Recalls the details of a process in the right order.

8.3 ☐ Recalls regular routines but needs reminding about those that are less familiar.

8.4 ☐ Finds it difficult to remember facts, instructions or routines.

8.5 ☐ Soon forgets any information given formally or informally.

9.0 Making judgements

9.1 ☐ Makes well-reasoned judgements based on all the available evidence.

9.2 ☐ Recognizes bias and unsupported arguments.

9.3 ☐ Normally distinguishes between fact and opinion.

9.4 ☐ Finds it difficult to distinguish between fact and opinion.

9.5 ☐ Sometimes shows bias and makes ill-founded judgements.

9.6 ☐ Does not usually make objective judgements.

10.0 Using evidence
10.1 ☐ Makes interpretations and predictions based on observed evidence.
10.2 ☐ Is prepared to look for explanations of observed evidence.
10.3 ☐ Makes accurate observations.
10.4 ☐ Has difficulty in making accurate observations.
10.5 ☐ Does not easily distinguish between relevant and irrelevant evidence.
10.6 ☐ Has difficulty in using evidence appropriately to support an interpretation or point of view.

11.0 Visual interpretation (symbols, charts, tables, drawings)
11.1 ☐ Expresses complicated ideas in visual form.
11.2 ☐ Understands ideas represented in visual form.
11.3 ☐ Finds it difficult to understand ideas represented by symbols, charts, tables or drawings.
11.4 ☐ Understands everyday signs.
11.5 ☐ Has difficulty in understanding any form of visual display.

12.0 Creative skills
12.1 ☐ Design work shows originality and appreciation of the potential of a number of different materials.
12.2 ☐ Is particularly interested in creative activities in a variety of media.
12.3 ☐ Design work is original and exciting but poor application spoils the quality of the final product.
12.4 ☐ Responds enthusiastically when guided towards creative activity but is not greatly interested in expressing own ideas.
12.5 ☐ Has shown only occasional interest in most creative activities.
12.6 ☐ Displays little interest in becoming involved in creative activity and his/her work lacks originality and imagination.
12.7 ☐ Attempts practical work conscientiously, but copies rather than creates.

13.0 Manual skills
13.1 ☐ Works with dexterity and precision.
13.2 ☐ Consistently produces an acceptable standard of work.
13.3 ☐ With guidance works accurately.
13.4 ☐ Finds it difficult to produce accurate work manually.
13.5 ☐ Is rather clumsy and this is reflected in the low standard of work produced.

14.0 Numerical skills
14.1 ☐ Consistently solves complex problems by a variety of methods.

14.2 ☐ Solves problems involving the use of decimals, fractions and percentages.

14.3 ☐ Copes successfully with those problems which can be solved by using calculations with whole numbers.

14.4 ☐ Recognizes and uses place value correctly.

14.5 ☐ Can solve problems requiring simple addition, subtraction or multiplication.

14.6 ☐ Requires help to solve accurately simple problems involving whole numbers.

14.7 ☐ Has considerable difficulty in working accurately with numbers even with assistance.

15.0 Mental calculations

15.1 ☐ Makes accurate mental calculations in a way which is appropriate to his/her level of numerical ability.

15.2 ☐ Is able to do mental calculations with whole numbers involving addition, subtraction or multiplication.

15.3 ☐ Can cope with very basic mental arithmetic.

15.4 ☐ Does not make accurate mental calculations.

16.0 Cross-checking

16.1 ☐ Makes realistic estimations for cross-checking purposes.

16.2 ☐ Finds accurate estimations of length and area difficult to achieve.

16.3 ☐ Does not make realistic estimations of length and area.

17.0 Measuring

17.1 ☐ Accurately uses a wide variety of finely graduated measuring instruments.

17.2 ☐ Accurately uses everyday measuring instruments.

17.3 ☐ Requires some assistance in the accurate use of everyday measuring instruments.

17.4 ☐ Does not use measuring equipment accurately even with assistance.

18.0 Use of calculators

18.1 ☐ Uses a calculator in a way which is appropriate to his/her level of numerical ability.

19.0 Microcomputer skills

19.1 ☐ Effectively uses appropriate computing techniques to solve problems.

19.2 ☐ Competently uses a commercial computer package, e.g. Database; Word-Processor; Spread Sheet.

19.3 ☐ Uses and responds to a straightforward computer program.

19.4 ☐ With assistance can use and responds to a straightforward computer program.

19.5 ☐ Has acquired few keyboard skills and is not able to use a computer for educational purposes.

19.6 ☐ Sometimes uses a computer to play games.

20.0 Ability in a foreign language

20.1 ☐ Participates with ease in conversation with native speakers.

20.2 ☐ Understands the gist of conversations between native speakers.

20.3 ☐ Speaks and understands well enough to communicate in everyday situations.

20.4 ☐ Speaks and understands short sentences and questions.

20.5 ☐ Understands commonly used words.

20.6 ☐ Finds difficulty in remembering and using any words in a foreign language.

20.7 ☐ Shows little interest or ability in acquiring foreign language skills.

PARENTS' PAGE AND PUPIL PAGE RELATING TO ACTIVITIES OUT OF SCHOOL

Parents' page

When you have read your child's Record of Achievement we hope that you will write some comments. You may agree or disagree with what has been written. Both sorts of comments are valuable to the school, so please do not hesitate to write what you really think.

1. How do you feel about your child's progress? Do you think his/her needs are being met?

2. Please write your comments on anything that has been written about your child that you strongly agree with.

3. Please write your comments on anything that you strongly disagree with.

4. Are there any particular problems you would like to draw attention to?

5. Have there been any changes in your child's home or personal circumstances that you would like to discuss with the school in confidence?

Yes   No
☐   ☐   **If YES, someone from school will be in touch.**

6. Are there any other comments you would like to make? Please write them on the back of this page.

Signature (Parents/Guardians) _____
Date _____

Out of school

Comments

☐ You manage to get yourself up in good time
☐ You need a lot of calling and then have to rush around

	Yes	No
You make your bed and leave your room tidy:	☐	☐

You help with:	Yes	Sometimes	No
Washing up	☐	☐	☐
Cleaning jobs	☐	☐	☐
Repair jobs	☐	☐	☐
Family wash	☐	☐	☐
Shopping	☐	☐	☐
Cooking meals	☐	☐	☐
Gardening	☐	☐	☐

☐ You have prepared a full meal for yourself
☐ You have cooked yourself a hot snack
☐ You make a good cup of tea or coffee

☐ You plan very carefully over a period what you want to
do with all your money
☐ You may plan to buy something special, but you are
usually quite casual with money
☐ You spend your money as soon as you get it
☐ You always get your homework done without needing to
be told
☐ You have to be nagged to get down to your homework
☐ You'll do anything to avoid your homework
When staying away from home:
☐ You prefer to be with your family
☐ You prefer to be with a group of other young people
☐ If you give your word that you'll do something, you
always do it
☐ You always mean to keep promises, but you sometimes
don't carry them out
☐ You often forget to do things you've promised
☐ You know where these are:

	Yes	No
Family Doctor	☐	☐
Chemist	☐	☐
Post Office	☐	☐
Public Library	☐	☐
Swimming Pool	☐	☐

You seem to enjoy yourself living away from the family
for a few days and don't get homesick:

Yes	No
☐	☐

REFERENCES

Andrews, S. (1988) *Robert Arthur Essex Leaves School*. London: The Industrial Society.

Ashforth, D. (1990) *Records of Achievement in the Market Place*. Windsor: NFER-Nelson.

Brennan, S. (1988) *A User Perspective on Records of Achievement*. Research and Consultancy Service, Report No. 14. The Northern Ireland Council for Educational Research.

Bridges, D. (1989) Pupil assessment from the perspective of naturalistic research. In H. Simons and J. Elliott (eds) *Rethinking Appraisal and Assessment*. Milton Keynes: Open University Press.

Broadfoot, P. (1982) The pros and cons of profiles, *Forum* 24 (3), 66–9.

Broadfoot, P. (ed.) (1986) *Profiles and Records of Achievement. A Review of Issues and Practice*. London: Holt.

Broadfoot, P. (1987) *Introducing Profiling: a Practical Manual*. London: Macmillan.

Burchell, H. (1987) School leaving profiles for lower attaining pupils. Is there a role?, *Educational Review* 39 (3): 231–45.

Burgess, R., Evans, K., Pole, C. and Priestley, C. (1991) *The Warwickshire Records of Achievement Project: Issues and Themes*. University of Warwick.

Burgess, T. and Adams, E. (1985) *Records of Achievement at 16*. Slough: NFER-Nelson.

Burgess, T. and Adams, E. (1986) Records for all at 16. In P. Broadfoot (ed.) *Profiles and Records of Achievement: A Review of Issues and Practice*. London: Holt.

Confederation of British Industry (1980) Records of Achievement: the CBI view. *Education and Training Bulletin* 10 (3) August. London: CBI.

Confederation of British Industry (1983) *Records of Achievement – The CBI View*. London: CBI.

Crouch, C. (1979) *The Politics of Industrial Relations*. Glasgow: Collins/Fontana.

Dale, R., Bowe, R., Harris, D. *et al.* (1990) *The TVEI Story: Policy, Practice and Preparation for the Workforce*. Milton Keynes: Open University Press.

Department of Education and Science (1984) *Records of Achievement: A Statement of Policy*. London: DES/Welsh Office.

Department of Education and Science (1985) *Better Schools*. London: HMSO.

Department of Education and Science (1991) *Circular 66/91*. London: HMSO.

Eggleston, J. (1984) School examinations – some sociological issues. In P. Broadfoot (ed.) *Selection Certification and Control: Social Issues in Educational Assessment*. Lewes: Falmer Press.

Evans, K. (1989) *Records of Achievement in Warwickshire: A Case Study of Fourways School*. Warwick: University of Warwick: CEDAR Report.

Evans, M. (1988) *Practical Profiling*. London: Routledge.

Fairbairn, D. (1988) Pupil profiling: new approaches to recording and reporting achievement. In R. Murphy and H. Torrance (eds) *The Changing Face of Educational Assessment*. Milton Keynes: Open University Press.

Garforth, D. and Macintosh, H. (1986) *Profiling, A User's Manual*. Cheltenham: Thornes.

Gleeson, D. (ed.) (1987) *TVEI and Secondary Education*. Milton Keynes: Open University Press.

Goacher, B. and Reid, M. (1984) *School Reports to Parents*. Windsor: NFER-Nelson.

Hall, G. (1989) *Records of Achievement: Issues and Practice*. London: Kogan Page.

Hargreaves, A., Baglin, E., Henderson, P., Leeson, P. and Tossell, T. (1988) *Personal and Social Education: Choices and Challenges*. Oxford: Blackwell.

Hinckley, S., Pole, C., Sims, D. and Stoney, S. (1987) *The TVEI Experience: Views from Teachers and Students*. Sheffield: MSC.

Hicks, J. (1986) Pupil profiling and the secondary school, *Educational Review* 38 (1).

Hitchcock, G. (1986a) Instituting profiling within a school. In P. Broadfoot

(1986) (ed.) *Profiles and Records of Achievement: A Review of Issues and Practice*. London: Cassell.

Hitchcock, G. (1986b) *Profiles and Profiling a Practical Introduction*. London: Longman.

ILEA (1988) *The London Record of Achievement*. London: ILEA Central Assessment Team.

James, M. (1989a) Negotiation and dialogue in student assessment and teacher appraisal. In H. Simons and J. Elliott (eds) *Rethinking Appraisal and Assessment*. Milton Keynes: Open University Press.

James, M. (1989b) *Evaluation for Policy: Rationality and Political Reality: The Paradigm Case of PRAISE?* Paper presented at CEDAR Conference on Educational Research and Evaluation for Policy and Practice, September. University of Warwick.

Law, B. (1988) *Uses and Abuses of Profiling a Handbook on Reviewing and Recording Student Experience and Achievement*. London: Paul Chapman.

Mansell, J. (1984) *A Burst of Interest in Profiles*. London: FEU Curriculum Review and Development Unit.

Meighan, R. (1977) Pupils' perceptions of the classroom technique of post-graduate student teachers, *British Journal of Teacher Education* 3 (2): 139–48.

Moon, B. (1990) *New Curriculum – National Curriculum*. London: Hodder and Stoughton.

Munby, S. (1989) *Assessing and Recording Achievement*. Oxford: Blackwell.

Newsom, J. (1963) *Half our Future: A report of the Central Advisory Council for Education*. London: DES/HMSO.

Norwood, (1941) *Report of the Committee of the Secondary Examinations Council*. London: HMSO.

Orwell, G. (1949) *Nineteen Eighty-Four*. London: Secker and Warburgh.

Pearson, R. and Pike, G. (1989) *Employers' Demands for Young People*. Brighton: Institute of Manpower Studies.

Phillips, P. (1989) Recording personal achievement – a critique. In S. Munby (ed.) *Assessing and Recording Achievement*. Oxford: Blackwell.

Pole, C. (1989) *Records of Achievement in Warwickshire: Benton School: A Case Study*. Warwick: University of Warwick: CEDAR Report.

Pole, C. (1990) *Records of Achievement and the Employer: A Report to Coventry LEA*. Warwick: University of Warwick: CEDAR Report.

Pole, C. (1991) *Records of Achievement in Warwickshire: Herbert Marshall School: A Case Study*. Warwick: University of Warwick: CEDAR Report.

PRAISE (1987) *Pilot Records of Achievement in Schools Evaluation – an Interim Report*. London: DES/Welsh Office.

PRAISE (1988) *Report of the Pilot Records of Achievement in Schools Evaluation*. London: DES/Welsh Office.

Priestley, C. (1990) *Records of Achievement in Warwickshire: Rowan Hill School – a case study*. Warwick: University of Warwick: CEDAR Report.

Records of Achievement National Steering Committee (RANSC) (1989) *Records of Achievement: Report of the Records of Achievement National Steering Committee*. London: DES/Welsh Office.

Ryrie, A., Furst, A. and Lauder, M. (1979) *Choices and Chances*. Sevenoaks: Hodder and Stoughton.

Saunders, M. (1986) The innovative enclave: Unintended effects of TVEI implementation. In R. Fiddy and I. Stronach (eds) *TVEI Working Papers 1*. Norwich: CARE, University of East Anglia.

Scott, D. (1989) *Coursework and Coursework Assessment in the GCSE*. Warwick: University of Warwick: CEDAR Report.

Simon, B. (1988) *Bending the Rules: The Baker 'reform' of Education*. London: Lawrence and Wishart.

Sims, D. (1987) Work experience in TVEI: Students' views and reactions – A preliminary study. In S. Hinckley, C. Pole, D. Sims and S. Stoney (eds) *The TVEI Experience*. Sheffield: MSC.

Skinsley, M. (1986) Profiling using the computer, *Bulletin of Physical Education* 22 (3): 48–51.

Spooner, R. (1983) A celebration of success or an advertisement of inadequacy, *Education* 162 (2): 29.

Stansbury, D. (1985) *Programme to Develop Records of Experience as an Element in the Documentation of School Leavers*. Report on the preliminary phase. March 1984–July 1985. Totnes: Springline Trust.

Stoney, S., Pole, C. and Sims, D. (1986) *The Management of TVEI*. Sheffield: MSC.

Stronach, I. (1989) A critique of the 'new assessment': from currency to carnival? In H. Simons and J. Elliott (eds) *Rethinking Appraisal and Assessment*. Milton Keynes: Open University Press.

Swales, T. (1979) *Record of Personal Achievement: An Independent Evaluation of the Swindon RPA Scheme*. Schools Council Pamphlet.

Torrance, H. (1988) *Records of Achievement and Formative Assessment: Some Complexities of Practice*. Paper presented at British Educational Research Association Annual Conference, September. University of East Anglia.

Turner, G. (1990) *External Local Evaluation of the Dorset Record of Achievement Project YTS Extension: A Second Report*. Southampton: Assessment and Evaluation Unit, Southampton University.

Woods, P. (1983) *Sociology and the School*. London: Routledge and Kegan Paul.

INDEX